VEDUCATED!

An Educator's Guide for Vegan-Inclusive Teaching

VEDUCATED!

An Educator's Guide for Vegan-Inclusive Teaching

Laura Chepner

2020

Danvers

Vegan Publishers™

Vegan Publishers
Danvers, Massachusetts
www.veganpublishers.com

Front cover design by Gawk Designs
Typesetting by Nicola May Design

ISBN: 978-1-940184-62-3

CONTENTS

Dedication

Lois Rae – you are my sunshine, thank you.
Martin – my love, thank you.

To Sam and our supportive and loving parents, Bernice and
Gerry, you're all diamonds, thank you.

FOREWORD

Today, school children the world over express their bitter disillusionment with the legacy the adult world is leaving them. From calamitous climate change to mass extinction of biodiversity, adults have put in jeopardy the very lives of those they love the most – their children.

In some way, though, the collapse of so much that humanity has depended upon for centuries has the potential to bring us together in a single-minded common purpose to do what we have to do to make it right. Together we must take responsibility, each of us individually, to heal our earth and do justice to the animals who share life's journey with us.

It starts with the wisdom in that old axiom "you are what you eat." By eliminating the violence inherent in the massive meat trade, we take the first step in redefining humanity, liberating not only the animals that suffer for our choice of food, but liberating ourselves too from the burden that comes hand-in-hand with the role of the oppressor. In this way we can slowly rebuild the world we want for those who come after us – the children.

Veducated! takes us on this journey, step by liberating step, bringing hope and health back into the classroom, and a sense of pride in who we are as humans.

Louise van der Merwe
Managing Trustee of the Humane Education Trust, Editor at Animal Voice, Director of both Animal Voice Academy and Caring Classrooms, and South Africa's representative at Compassion in World Farming

"Teacher competencies are understood to include skills, knowledge and understanding, as well as values and moral sensibilities, and professional identity. Teaching competencies associated with change agency are broadly conceptualised to include relevant knowledge and understanding as well a capacity to engage with educational change and reflect on one's own beliefs and values. Preparing teachers as agents of change to promote social justice and inclusion requires clarity not only about what teachers need to know, do and believe but how they will exercise their agency as teachers when adopting this approach."

–Nataša Pantić and Lani Florian[1]

INTRODUCTION

"If this is the year [2018] of mainstream Veganism, as every trend forecaster and market analyst seem to agree, then there is not one single cause, but a perfect plant-based storm of factors."

–Dan Hancox[2]

In 2018, 3.5 million people, 7% of the UK population, identified as being vegan.[3] That's a staggering increase of 700% since 2016, when only 1% identified as such. With these numbers on the rise, showing no indication of slowing down any time soon, schools up and down the country, and around the world, are guaranteed to see a rise in their vegan intake; that is if they haven't already. This is the first of many books to come on education, inclusion, and veganism, and even if you yourself may not be participating in this social justice movement, there is no denying that it is occurring.

Over the last two years, whilst writing this guidebook, there have been countless vegan-related societal changes, so much so that I have had to add to, and edit my, writing relentlessly. Major food chains have incorporated vegan lines into their global menus, debates and discussions have been held almost daily on TV and radio, and Canada has decided to remove dairy milk from their national nutritional information. As I write this, on this very day, there will have been quotes and articles published globally which make the above statistics seem outdated already. One person really can make a difference, as the ripples of all of the separate individuals campaigning and advocating for veganism, who were once viewed as insignificant, are now converging and making waves. It has been quite phenomenal watching the growth of veganism from the inside looking outwards. But, for those who are not vegan and looking from the outside inwards, the perception may be that this growth is a trend or a fad which may pass. Yet over a quarter of a million people around the world signed up for Veganuary 2019, an initiative which encourages people to "try veganism" for a month, with much larger numbers expected in 2020. It may very well be time to accept that veganism is here to stay. The more you understand it, the easier you will find your interactions with vegans within society.

I decided to go vegan in 2014, a choice that I made whilst weaning my daughter from breast milk to solids when she was around seven months old. At that time, I was a teacher and newly promoted Special Educational Needs Coordinator (Senco) on maternity leave with plenty of spare time to read and research my new lifestyle. I found it quite easy, having already been vegetarian for many years, yet eye opening, heartbreaking, liberating, and incredibly exciting all at the same time. In saying that, it was and still is the best decision that I have ever made. Throughout my maternity leave, I had every intention of returning to my vocational profession with just as much gusto and passion that I had when I had temporarily left it. I adored the school where I worked and didn't think that I would ever leave; I was very excited to go back to work after my maternity leave was over. I enjoyed the challenges that my position as Senco brought and had genuinely missed the children (a feeling that some other teachers will find hard to believe, but it is true). Slowly but surely, as I re-immersed myself back into the world of teaching, I unfortunately found that my ethics began to clash with the curriculum and ethos at the school. As I was slowly eradicating animal use from my own life, I found that the environment in which I was working subtly promoted the use of animals every day and in every which way. So, I left.

I was now deeply invested in veganism and I had no choice but to move in a different direction. I decided to open a vegan restaurant in 2015, Lolo's, having had some experience working as a bar and restaurant supervisor part-time during my four-year degree in primary education. It was a tough gig being a company director, tougher than I could ever have imagined (nothing to do with veganism, just the nature of the beast). I had my restaurant for three years and I enjoyed receiving emails from grateful customers who took the leap to veganism off the back of my restaurant's existence, which made the whole endeavour worthwhile. But, it wasn't for me. I sold my restaurant around the time my daughter started school and realised my life's purpose. I quickly experienced just how excluded vegan children can feel in our current education system. I realised that a vegan school consultancy business was the perfect way to marry my first passion of teaching and my newfound passion of veganism. I wanted to get into schools and explain what veganism was and why it was important that the children, but especially the teachers, knew what veganism was too. The further along you travel through this guidebook the more you will understand my necessity for this urgency. This thought solidified in my mind after having sat at a table with ten female teachers during my last full-time working week and realising that not one of them knew that a cow, like us, had to be pregnant in order to produce milk.

After doing a decent amount of research, I discovered that there were in fact zero vegan-inclusive education consultants in the UK and possibly the world. Having gained the extra skills that came with being a Company Director under my belt, my new consultancy firm Primary Veducation was born in 2017. There needed to be some way of feeding this valuable information into our schools in order that our educators become better informed.

My first task with Primary Veducation was to push for vegan food at my daughter's school as, unbelievably at the time of initial intake, we were denied this option. I started helping other parents in similar situations and began to think that there should be a universal guidebook; a book from which teachers can learn what topics or language could result in making vegan children feel excluded and provide ideas around helping these kids feel included instead. The Conservative Government at the time had much bigger issues to deal with, such as Brexit, so realistically I knew that pushing for a vegan-inclusion policy was likely to be at the bottom of the pile along with potholes and bin collection conversations. As I knew that I couldn't depend on the Department for Education to listen, or to take me seriously, I started typing away to create what I believed to be a useful resource that any teacher could refer to for guidance.

As I write this, my daughter is currently in Reception (ages 4-5) and I know from my volunteer work at her school that she is hurtling towards unsuitable topics in Year 1 (ages 5-6). Time is of the essence; I need my daughter's future teacher to read this guidebook. If I need it to exist so desperately, then I can guarantee that many other vegan parents need it to exist too.

Who is this Guidebook for?

This guidebook has been written with the inclusive teacher in mind, the kind of teacher who goes to great lengths to ensure that each child in their classroom makes progress, feels valued, and most importantly, feels understood. Those teachers, like me, who would make a point of looking at every one of their thirty plus children directly in the eyes at morning registration, sincerely acknowledging each individual at least once, just in case there isn't enough time to invest in them again during the rest of the busy day ahead.

The fact of the matter is, and you will understand this more once you have read the first chapter, the vegan child sees the world through completely different eyes than the majority who choose to be omnivores. The vegan child has a vastly different belief system and moral compass than most others in society. They are currently a minority and mostly misunderstood. Their viewpoints are deeply important to them and very much worth taking into consideration, as you would with any other child who has specific needs. As an inclusive school, and more specifically an inclusive teacher, you should want to know more about their lives and beliefs so that you can tailor your practice to creating a learning environment in which all of your children, vegan children included, can feel comfortable and thrive.

This guidebook is also intended for parents of vegan children who may wish to gift it to their children's teacher. You might feel as though your child is learning, cared for, and accepted at school, but maybe not fully understood, or differentiated for, in an academic sense simply because the classroom teacher is unaware of the intricacies involved in living a vegan lifestyle. If you are a teacher who has received this book from a parent, please do not be offended or dismiss this gift. There is no judgement here; there is however a lot of useful information that will inevitably create a better atmosphere for learning. What teacher wouldn't want that?

What are the Aims of this Guidebook?

This guidebook has been written with a number of intentions. Firstly, I aim to explain, in its simplest form, what veganism is to an interested, albeit slightly apprehensive audience, without any criticism directed towards you. You will not be expected to make any personal lifestyle changes. Although admittedly vegans always hope that their advocacy will inevitably lead to more vegans, the vegan child in your class is at the centre of this guidebook. You will become aware that, as a teacher, you are expected to know and understand the lives of those you teach. In Chapter 1, I cover the main reasons as to why a child or family may have chosen the vegan lifestyle. For each individual or family, the reasons may be different, and there may be more than one. I believe there are four main categories – Animal Rights, Health, The Environment, and Compassion – and I would bet my life on the fact that all vegans will refer to at least one of those reasons when asked why they made the switch. These four categories make up the first chapter's subheadings.

Secondly, although no personal lifestyle changes are required, another intention for this book is that you will gain the knowledge and confidence necessary to tweak your teaching practice and become as vegan-inclusive as you can be whilst at work. In Chapter 2, I provide hints, tips, ideas, and vegan-inclusive topic plans so that you have the tools and support readily available to become a vegan-inclusive teacher. Don't be afraid to ask questions of the vegan child as well as referring to Chapter 2 as often as is necessary. Until the suggestions outlined here become second nature to you, and as with all habitual changes, it will take time and practise.

A classroom that takes the vegan viewpoint into consideration, adds to the multicultural, multilingual, and mixed ability differentiation that is already taking place. In Chapter 3, I move away from the individual vegan child's viewpoint, take a look at the overall benefits of adopting a vegan-inclusive classroom, and how it has the potential to improve the ethos of your entire school and wider community.

My final intention is to encourage a harmonious and inclusive teaching and learning environment which goes just a little bit further in celebrating the diversity within your classroom. Chapter 4 includes lesson plans enabling you to teach the children in the class about veganism at a point when you are vegan-inclusive confident. Bringing peers into the picture and providing them with an opportunity to celebrate their friend's vegan lifestyle is the final piece of the fully inclusive puzzle.

Though examples provided in this guidebook are primarily focused on primary education, as this is the area in which I have spent most of my adult working life, the knowledge and skills gained here can easily be transferred to secondary schools, higher education, further education, or even the workplace. The themes and messages in this guidebook are easily digestible, factual, and relevant and can be transferred across the continents. Having a true understanding of what veganism is, and then implementing some simple changes to your language and behaviour, can make a vegan person of any age, and in any area of society, feel included and respected. We are all in this together.

CHAPTER 1:

Why Should You Make your Environment More Inclusive for Vegan Children?

~~~~~~

"Inclusive Education is a process involving changes in the way schools are organised, in the curriculum and in teaching strategies, to accommodate the range of needs and abilities among pupils."

–Judy Sebba[4]

Throughout this chapter, you will learn the key reasons why a family or an individual chooses to adopt the vegan lifestyle. Although you yourself might not be vegan or place value on the following viewpoints, it is of the highest importance that you understand the vegan perspective so that you can try, at the very least, to relate to the vegan child in your setting. I remember, as Newly Qualified Teacher (NQT), being part of a staff meeting that centred on inclusivity for children who were partially sighted. Throughout that meeting, we wore glasses over our eyes which were blurred to var-

⅃s degrees, demonstrating what partially sighted children in our school were able, or unable, to access on a whiteboard. We were able to genuinely empathise and then plan accordingly, having seen the world, literally, through their eyes. I write this chapter with the same intention. You may never be vegan, but if you begin to see the world though a vegan child's eyes, with this new perspective, you'll feel more confident in making the necessary, and often simple changes to your practice.

At this point the most important question to ask is, **what is Veganism?**

You may have been told by your school administration team that you have a vegan child joining you in September and the first thought that came into your mind may very well have been, "...a what?" Or you may have heard some negative connotations or passing comments about veganism on the television before, laughed, and then dismissed them as irrelevant, until now. Veganism is not a weird cult, as the mainstream media may have depicted it in the past, a religion, or a hippie phase that your vegan child may be going through. In fact, it is a deep, conscious, exciting lifestyle choice and social justice movement that is based on a marriage of compassion and facts. The Vegan Society defines veganism as follows:[5]

> "A philosophy and way of living which seeks to exclude—as far as is possible and practicable—all forms of **exploitation of, and cruelty to, animals** for food, clothing or any other purpose; and by extension, promotes the development and use of animal-free alternatives for the **benefit of humans, animals** and the **environment**. In dietary terms it denotes the practice of dispensing with all products derived wholly or partly from animals."

Using the Vegan Society's definition of veganism, we can look closely at each of the main reasons for a person's commitment to this way of living. Let's start by exploring what is probably the most common reason, the **"...exploitation of, and cruelty to, animals."**

Animal Rights

"Being kind to animals is not enough. Avoiding cruelty is not enough. Housing animals in more comfortable, larger cages is not enough. Whether we exploit animals to eat, to wear, to entertain us, or to learn, the truth of animal rights requires empty cages, not larger cages."

–Tom Regan[6]

Land Animals Used for Food

One of the key reasons for a family or individual to become vegan, is the belief that all animals are equal and do not deserve to be tortured and killed unnecessarily for food. This is not a new concept; many of our most notable historical figures chose this lifestyle including Leonardo da Vinci, Plato, Voltaire, Martin Luther King, Rosa Parks, Ghandi, Susan Anthony, and Albert Einstein.

The vegan child will be acutely aware of the process that farmed animals go through, from birth to death, and how each industry has its own way of maximising profits at the expense of the animal in question. I have omitted the gore from this guidebook is so as not to scare you off too soon, but there are recommended video links in the resources section at the end of the guidebook which will explain the brutal practices in each of these industries. Although I am an advocate for sharing torture practices that are rife within the animal agricultural industries on personal social media platforms, I am also acutely aware of my target audience for this guidebook. That being said, you should keep in mind that all vegans associate animal farms with nothing but cruelty and exploitation and therefore, will not see them as the happy places that the marketing companies portray them as.

You may have previously visited local farms or petting pens on a school trip or with your own children, but these supposedly happy and family friendly small farms are, in the vast minority, and the animals always die an early, ugly death in the end. The reality of how the majority of animal farms function is at the complete other end of the spectrum. Thousands of animals are housed together in sheds that use unnatural lighting and unsanitary cages, where the animals are bored and neglected and these giant factory farms tend to be built way out in the countryside so that public access is limited.

According to a 2019 report, "There are currently almost 800 U.S.-style 'Megafarms' in the U.K., and since 2011, the number of intensive pig and poultry farms has increased by 26 percent, an investigation revealed. The largest farms hold more than a million chickens, 20,000 pigs, or 2,000 dairy cows. (Poultry is by far the biggest sector, comprising 86 percent of the permit-holding intensive operations.)"[7]

In this modern era, social media has enabled accessibility to footage of how farmed animals are treated so people, including children, can make informed decisions about whether they wish to contribute to those industries or not. Your vegan child may or may not have seen these videos (my daughter hasn't), but they can imagine what it must be like for their little friends trapped in these industries. As far as vegans are concerned, "the laughing cow" or "happy egg" campaigns are a complete fallacy created by well-paid marketing companies.

Vegetarians

I became vegetarian at the age of 11 after asking my Grandma Wynn why her sandwich was called "tongue"? As soon as she replied, "Because it is an actual tongue," I never ate meat again. So that there is no confusion as to what a vegetarian will or won't eat, here is the definition of vegetarian according to the Oxford Dictionary: "A person who does not eat meat or fish."[8] Personally,

I connected the dots after my Grandmother's explanation and was heartbroken to think that a gentle cow had died for a sandwich. Two decades later my heart broke even more as I realised how babies in the dairy industry were treated and I have never knowingly eaten animal products since. I have evolved from an omnivore to a vegetarian, and now to a vegan and feel qualified enough to say that veganism and vegetarianism are in fact completely different lifestyles. Although they get clumped together on menus, the difference between them is stark, even more so, I believe, than the difference between an omnivore and a vegetarian. The exploitation that goes into creating eggs and dairy for consumption is phenomenal.

The dairy and egg industries kill billions of animals worldwide. They are not a by-product of the meat industry, which is why vegetarians, although doing their small bit by omitting meat, are still consumers of the animal agricultural industry. On dairy farms cows have to be pregnant, just like us, in order to produce milk. They repeatedly endure artificially inseminated pregnancies only to give birth and then almost immediately their newborn calves are separated from their mothers. I found this specific piece of information out as I was breastfeeding my own newborn and my heart ached for those mothers who have their maternal bonds broken so that humans can drink their "breast" milk instead of their babies. Female reproductive organs are exploited and, depending on the sex of the newborn, they may well not live past their second day. On a dairy farm, for example, male calves can't produce milk as they grow older. They are deemed as a waste product and disposed of or made into "veal". The females will live a similar life to their mothers in that they will have several births until they collapse from exhaustion and then it is off to the slaughterhouse she goes. Similarly, on an egg farm, male chicks are disposed of by gassing, grinding, suffocating or drowning as they will never be able to produce eggs and become profitable. The female hens will go on to live a similar life to their mother, who they have never met, and be cramped into a cage to produce eggs. That is until she can no longer produce eggs and it is off to the slaughterhouse she goes. Interestingly, it is because of these practices, which take advantage of female reproductive organs, that a lot of feminists are joining the vegan movement.

The main difference between vegetarianism and veganism is committing to, and actioning on, the belief that every single living being on this planet no matter how big or small deserves a life free from oppression and discrimination. If you see a cow as more important than a monkey, or a turtle as more important than a shrimp, then you are actively classifying animals into categories. Some animals are seen as pets while other animals are seen as food. The line down the middle which creates this distinction is put there by the industries that breed them for profit. These categories aren't real; they are social constructs that are based on convenience and greed. Veganism accepts that cows, monkeys, turtles, and shrimps are equal, have their own part to play on this planet, and should be left, without interference, to fulfil their own purpose and freely live their lives. A word that may be new to you, but one that vegans have been using to describe how animals are categorised and then discriminated against, is "speciesism."

Encyclopaedia Britannica describes speciesism as follows:[9]

> "Speciesism as in applied ethics and the philosophy of animal rights, the practice of treating members of one species as morally more important than members of other species; also, the belief that this practice is justified. The notion has been variously formulated in terms of the interests, rights, and personhood of humans and animals and in terms of the supposed moral relevance of species membership."

The term speciesism was introduced by the English philosopher Richard Ryder in the 1970s and brought further into our consciousness by the Australian philosopher Peter Singer who said:[10]

> "Animals can suffer. So, insofar as they have the capacity for suffering, they too have interests (for instance, they have an interest in not being tortured). But, if the interests of all individuals should be given moral consideration, then animals too should be given moral consideration. Failing to do so is 'speciesism.'"

As an example, speciesism is when someone eating a beef hamburger feels that they have the right to be disgusted by the Yulin dog meat eating festival. Speciesism is also the viewpoint of someone being horrified by those who enjoy eating snails, whilst they themselves are biting down on kangaroo meat. Once we take away cultural "norms," we begin to see these animals not as food but as individuals. This is where hypocrisy and discrimination ends and veganism begins.

Primary schools use animals as puppets and toys, on wall displays, and as a muse to teach various skills through. This is completely understandable, as children have known and loved animals from birth, when their first toys and best friends were their cuddly teddies, piggies, or bunnies. Therefore, it seems completely natural for teachers to capitalise on this and use what the children are both interested and invested in to keep them engaged. As well as this, I know that teachers have a lot of stress in their work and time is limited. Therefore, when there over three million resources available online to teach about "The Farm" it is no wonder that many teachers refer to and use these so that they feel they are not "reinventing the wheel." Are you perhaps starting to see the great contradiction? We claim to love our animal friends while we use their likenesses to teach, but actually we are selling a reality that is far from what these farmed animals experience in captivity. Speciesism is the first form of discrimination that our children are taught, whether it is taught consciously or unconsciously. Animal farm industries do not see animals as individuals; they see either profit or waste and every penny counts. The depiction of the joyful farm animal often used in primary schools is far from the painful truth. Children's author Ruby Roth wrote:[11]

> "Whether they live in the sunshine or a dark shed, all animals raised for meat and dairy are captured and killed in the end. Their deaths are violent and sad."

Sea Animals Used For Food

> "Fish is not a health food. Neither is it a magical wonder food that can guarantee good heart health and turn all kids into geniuses."
>
> –Dr. Justine Butler[12]

The present state of our oceans is desperately alarming. You may have heard about the effect that global climate change is having on our disappearing coral reefs, of which animal agriculture is a primary contributor. (Don't worry if you haven't, this will be covered in more depth later in the guidebook). You may have also read about the plastic pollution problem that is engulfing our waters. However, the media avoids mentioning the largest and most destructive threat to our aquatic life – fishing.

Due to our taste for seafood, the fishing industry is working harder than ever to keep up with demand, increasing year after year, for so many years now, that our oceans can hardly cope. The most frightening part is that the damage caused will soon, unless addressed, become irreversible, in our lifetime! According to the World Wildlife Fund, "85 percent of the world's fisheries are either fully exploited or overfished."[13]

There are several key issues relating to overfishing. Firstly, a key component is the missing elements in the food chain, as stated in an article on One Green Planet written By Arianna Pittman:[14]

> "Overfishing harms other marine life by disrupting the food chain, placing animals that rely on that species as a food source in danger of starvation. And when populations of predatory species are diminished, other species will overpopulate, destroying biodiversity, and causing the entire ecosystem to suffer."

Secondly, trawling, gillnets, and longlines used to catch fish are non-discriminative about who they catch and, because of this, millions of sea animals are caught and die and are then discarded as "bycatch." A 2014 report by Oceana described the state of affairs in just one part of the world as such, "300 whales and almost 700 sea turtles were entangled or killed in a single year in Atlantic and Gulf of Mexico longlines."[15]

Finally, trawling causes whole habitats to be ripped from the seabed destroying vast areas which are crucial to the survival of plant life and those who live and feed off it.

With an ever-growing human population, global warming, plastic pollution, and few restrictions placed upon the fishing industry, it does not look great for our aquatic friends. The vegan children in your class, especially if they are quite young, may not be fully aware of the environmental impact that eating fish is having on our already depleted eco-systems. They may choose not to eat fish purely because they think that they're cute, but there is no denying that if a vegan child in your class is fully aware of these issues, it is a deeply upsetting and somewhat frightening topic to have to accept as their reality and should be approached mindfully.

Honey

> "If the bee disappeared off the face of the earth, man would only have four years left to live."
> –Maurice Maeterlinck[16]

I have highlighted honey, which is actually bee vomit, as a standalone issue because of the fact that the bees' plight is not commonly known. In its simplest terms, the reason why honey is not vegan is that it is made by an animal. Vegans will not use anything that is made by an animal and that includes honey and beeswax. Bees spend their entire Spring and Summer working literally as, "busy bees," making and storing enough honey to see them through the colder months. Golden Blossom® Honey describes the process:[17]

> "In order to produce 1 pound of honey, 2 million flowers must be visited. A hive of bees must fly 55,000 miles to produce a pound of honey. One bee colony can produce 60 to 100 pounds of honey per year. An average worker bee makes only about 1/12 teaspoon of honey in its lifetime."

If humans extract the bees' hard-earned honey for themselves, it leaves the bees with an insufficient amount and they will die. The pesticides on plants and flowers do not help. It is true that bees are being killed numbering in the millions because of them, and if it was up to me, all plant-based food products would be organic, but honey extraction is the real problem. When bees are factory farmed, their honey is replaced by sugar syrup to prevent starvation but it severely lacks the nutrients held within real honey and does not sustain the colonies, not even close. Vegans know how vital this amazing flying insect is to our planet's entire ecosystem, as explained by poet Maurice Maeterlinck above, and choose plant alternatives such as agave, maple, or date syrup to sweeten their food.

Clothing and Materials

"A popular belief is that when something is known to be especially cruel, the product of that cruelty will be renounced and rejected by the masses. And often, it is refused by many. However, indulgence, naughtiness, sin, selfishness, shock, spectacle, transgression, and pursuits of clear markers of power are major driving forces within animal-based fashion industries like the luxury fashion market."

–Joshua Katcher[18]

Vegan children will refuse to use or wear products that have been taken, literally, off the backs of other earthlings. They wish to avoid silk, wool, fur, angora, down, leather, suede, cashmere, shearling, and other animal-derived clothing and products. The way that these materials are obtained include imprisonment, violence, and inevitably the death of the animals bred for this purpose. Sheep fight when being sheared, so farmers fight back too. Ducks fight when being plucked for down feathers, so farmers fight back too. Cows fight when being skinned alive, so farmers fight back too. There is a lot of violence; it is not a situation where any of these animals are grateful or willing. Vegan children empathise with the animals' perspectives and instead choose to wear faux and natural alternatives which are equally as effective. I will discuss in the next chapter ways to avoid these materials in your classroom and alternatives that the whole class can use when creating and designing.

The vegan child will be encouraged to know that the fur farm business is becoming quite outdated as major fashion houses such as Michael Kors, Jimmy Choo, Dior, and Versace all pledged to go fur-free in 2017, twenty-four years after Calvin Klein first made their pledge in 1994. Stella McCartney has also stated that since the brands' conception in 2001, she would never sell fur, and more importantly, that she will not sell animal skin leather or suede either, which is just as brutal for the animal but still widely used. Even high street shops are taking a look at changing consumer patterns with Zara, H&M, and Gap removing mohair from their shelves. Sustainable, environmentally-friendly, and ethical materials such as Piñatex pineapple leather are leading the way and fashionistas like Victoria Beckham and sports brand Adidas are inspired by vegan designers such as Joshua Katcher and Vaute Couture.

Animal Entertainment

"Is it because we have a hidden belief that animals don't suffer in the same way as humans?"
–Clare Mann[19]

Numeracy, literacy, and scientific skills are often taught through petting farms, zoos, circuses, safaris (in the UK), and aquariums. I have previously taught these topics myself and remember feeling grateful that there were already so many resources available to make planning easier. That being said, these topics will make the vegan child feel extremely uncomfortable and will trigger sadness at the thought of animals confined in cages and tanks rather than being free in their natural environment.

Petting farms, zoos, circuses, safaris, and aquariums exploit animals to create revenue. I use the word "exploit" specifically because the animals have no choice as to whether or not they want to be there. As a consequence, these animals are not only in completely unnatural and manmade habitats, but they are also overseen in a way that needs to be lucrative. It is as Jonathan

Safran Foer wrote in his exceptional book Eating Animals[20] in a chapter describing a poultry factory farm visit, "Every aspect of the chicken's lives had been engineered to produce more food for less cost."

It is the same in the animal entertainment industry. The smaller the cages and enclosures at any of the attractions listed above are, the cheaper they are to look after which can never be good for the animal.

Let's now further explore the everyday practises used in circus', zoos, safaris and aquariums. I've already provided an overview of animal farms, but wish to add a note on petting farms before this exploration.

The petting farms that you plan to visit, or who plan to visit you, are not a true representation of how working animal farms operate, so you may want to do some research. Then ask yourself, what are you really teaching the children by showing them a false version of that industry? And are you sending mixed messages by commenting on how cute these animals are, but then, an hour later at lunch, saying let's eat their friends? It is mindboggling to me as an adult, and must be amplified tenfold for a vegan child.

In 2017, Scotland officially banned the use of animals in the circus and thankfully, England is about to follow suit. This is a good thing, according to One Kind Planet:[21]

"For an animal, a life in the circus is a miserable one. Living conditions are cramped, badly maintained and lack the basic comforts animals need to be happy and healthy. They don't have the opportunity to exercise, socialise or exhibit any of their natural behaviours, instead spending their lives trapped in cages. Performances are loud, busy and stressful experiences and that's before they are forced to perform tricks. Training is cruel and revolves around punishment and fear, with animals beaten and whipped regularly. Animals kept in these environments are unhealthy; suffer from injuries, exhaustion and stress. Animals have also died from overheating in hot and cramped cages during transport between shows."

In 2017, *The Greatest Showman*, a film about the owner of the Ringling Bros. and Barnum & Bailey Circus decided to use computer animated animals. This was followed by the closure of the actual circus after 146 years, which speaks volumes. The vegan child believes that when attending the circus, the marvelling and awe should be directed towards the humans who willingly use their own bodies to entertain and hypnotise us.

The majority of children, and probably adults on a school trip to a UK safari park, will think that the animals there have plenty of room to move around as the area seems quite big to us. However, considering that Britain's largest safari park is 9,000 acres, in its entirety, how comfortable do you really think the elephants are? Global Sanctuary for Elephants explains:[22]

"When looking at wild elephants the size of their home range is staggering. The home range for wild African elephants can extend up to 11,000 square kilometres, more than 2.7 million acres, female Asian elephants, up to 400 square kilometres and almost double that for a male, up to 200,000 acres."

Hopefully you've gotten a sense by now as to why an individual may turn vegan from learning about the animal entertainment industry. However, you may still be thinking, "but they're only animals." If that's how you feel, fair enough, but what is vital is that you understand that the vegan child in your class loves and respects all animals equally and will feel the same emotions towards a pig, parrot, or porpoise in captivity as they would for your pet golden retriever if it were ever captured. Once you can get your head around that fact, vegan-inclusion will become easier to grasp. To the vegan child, there is no differentiation between species; they all deserve freedom.

People for the Ethical Treatment of Animals (PETA) enlightens us regarding aquatic life:[23]

> "Wild orcas and dolphins live in large, complex social groups and swim vast distances every day in the open ocean. In captivity, these animals can only swim in endless circles in tanks that are the equivalent of bathtubs, and they are denied the opportunity to engage in almost any natural behaviour. They are forced to perform meaningless tricks and often torn away from family members when they're shuffled between parks. Most die far short of their natural lifespans. Aquariums which exhibit marine life are tiny in comparison to the ocean that they were captured from. They are kept in tanks with various chemical and cleaning agents and expected to swim in the same circles over and over again for human amusement."

This is a distressing thought to the vegan child as they are able to empathise fully with the individuals who are trapped. The vegan child will be acutely aware that these animals are held against their will and that their captivity is masked, again, by clever marketing as "educational" or "animal conservation."

When these entertainment houses were first created, we lived in a world where seeing a tarantula, elephant, camel, or shark was an unimaginable event; that is unless you already lived in their homeland. In the Victorian age, trips to the zoo or circus to see these incredible creatures were truly remarkable and unforgettable experiences. It is easy to see how they became a worldwide and revered trend. The rise of the middle class, who had a "bob or two" to spend on family entertainment, looked for exciting ways to spend their hard-earned cash and knew very little of wild animals, their intelligence, or their social capabilities. Fast forward to the 21st century; we have learnt a great deal about animals and have access to information about them from numerous sources. Your one class visit is a few hours worth of excitement for you and the children, yet these sentient and perceptive individuals are in that caged environment twenty-four hours a day, away from their families, unable to act on instinctual behaviour, forced to make friendships with whomever they are placed with, and most importantly, they are completely denied their freedoms. By choosing this sort of trip, you are automatically excluding the vegan child who will have no choice but to refuse to attend; especially if animal entertainment was the catalyst for their veganism.

Should you still insist on visiting, the vegan child will also have to endure hearing about the trip for days after as their friends write recounts or draw pictures of the event extending the anguish and exclusion.

The vegan child will have watched Pixar's Finding Nemo and deeply felt for the fish, they will have cried during Disney's Dumbo as his mother was confronted with whips, ropes, and hooks, and they will have felt the pain of Marty as he yearned for open spaces and herds of other zebras in Dreamwork's Madagascar. Did you? If so, then you already believe in veganism.

In the next chapter I will discuss ways of teaching key skills through topics that are animal-centred and include trips that are also suitable for a vegan audience.

Further Animal Use

"Much like us, animals are sentient beings and aware of their feelings and emotions. Their lives matter to them and they have the same capacity to feel joy and pleasure, as well as pain and suffering."

–Sentient Beings | Rspca.Org.Uk[24]

On the whole, it's a pretty grim state of affairs for our fellow earthlings, and until the recent rise of veganism, these practices have been normalised and glorified, practically unquestioned for centuries.

And if all that isn't enough, there are animals that are manhandled in rodeos, painfully experimented on for science or cosmetics, exhausted to the point of death from racing, forcibly worked and practically broken from schlepping or carrying, tormented by matadors, preyed upon by poachers, hunters, or anglers, callously taught to fight until death, starved, captured, smuggled or sold into the unforgiving pet trade, interbred, neglected, euthanized, forgotten about, or left helpless as entire habitats have been demolished and entire species crawling towards extinction.

These are some of the ethical reasons a family or child may have become vegan. This overview will hopefully show you why it is important to have a vegan-inclusive classroom. These are deep and complex issues which the vegan child will be aware of and can sometimes be overwhelmed by when they think of how many billions of animals are used in these various ways.

You may very well be able to put this to the back of your mind and not be bothered at the situation that animals find themselves in, or a contradictory thought may resurface every now and then, but you are able to shake off those thoughts, as author and actor David Mitchell grapples with below. As a teacher though, it is well within your power to avoid references to those acts of violence whilst teaching and, for the sake of the vegan child, who can't easily expel those thoughts, it's of the highest importance that you do.

> "It's not uncommon, in the history of human societies, for things once deemed normal to start being deemed wrong. Sometimes it's something like homophobia, sometimes it's something like openly criticising those in power – it depends on the time and the society. Maybe all these vegans are harbingers of such a change. It annoys me because it makes me worry that I'm becoming a victim of history, just like all the animals I've eaten."[25]

Health

> "There are two kinds of cardiologists: vegans, and those who haven't read the data."
> –Kim Williams, M.D.[26]

Avoiding animal products to maintain a healthy way of living is another key reason why a child or family may have initially begun to head down the path to being vegan. The scientific community has begun to seriously focus on the long-term health benefits of a plant-based diet, with doctors across the globe prescribing a change in diet to eradicate our most common self-inflicted diseases, and in some cases replacing medicine altogether. Drs. Dean Ornish, Caldwell Esselstyn, Neal Barnard, Brooke Goldner, Pamela A. Popper, Michael Greger, Michael Klaper, John McDougal, and Milton Mills are some of the most outspoken physicians who support the view that a plant-based diet is the best way to eat for the prevention of, and healing of, the biggest diseases and killers of our time including heart disease, high blood pressure, obesity, some cancers, and type 2 diabetes.

I am highlighting the results from a handful of significant and recent studies to further explain this point. The conclusions are from scientists all over the world and cover a variety of diseases. I have specifically handpicked these cases to provide as much of an overview as possible without too much of the medical jargon. Should you wish to investigate further, references for these studies are included at the end of this book.

Epidemiologist Susanna Larsson of The National Institute of Environmental Medicine, Karolinska Institute, Stockholm observed after monitoring milk consumption in female volunteers that, "Our data indicates that high intakes of lactose and dairy products, particularly milk, are associated with an increased risk of serious ovarian cancer."[27]

Furthermore, in 2012, after researching both men and women at risk of stroke in a prospective cohort study they found that, "Results suggest that low-fat dairy consumption is inversely associated with the risk of stroke."[28]

The Department of Nutrition and Dietetics, at the University Kebangsaan, Malaysia found when researching asthmatic children that, "Results suggest that even over the short time period of eight weeks, an egg- and milk-free diet can reduce atopic symptoms and improve lung function in asthmatic children."[29]

Additionally, a team of researchers including H. S. Ghanim, Ph.D., Research Associate Professor for the Department of Medicine at the Jacobs School of Medicine and Biomedical Sciences, concluded in their study of inflammation and meat consumption that there was a "significantly higher increase in inflammation"[30] found in the subjects who had ingested just one animal-based meal. The typical Western diet is comprised of at least one animal-based ingredient in most daily meals and snacks. It begins to scream danger because as William Snyder wrote in *The Good, The Bad and The Ugly of Inflammation*:[31]

"When it's [Inflammation] good, it fights off foreign invaders, heals injuries and mops up debris. But when it's bad, inflammation ignites a long list of disorders: arthritis, asthma, atherosclerosis, blindness, cancer, diabetes and, quite possibly, autism and mental illness."

Another conclusion from a Cardiovascular Disease study conducted by Dr. Esselstyn[32] summarised quite astonishingly that:

"Most of the volunteer patients with CVD [Cardio Vascular Disease] responded to intensive counselling [in Plant-based nutrition], and those who sustained plant-based nutrition for a mean of 3.7 years experienced a low rate of subsequent cardiac events. Plant-based nutrition has the potential for a large effect on the CVD epidemic."

Considering that the vegan child will not have read these studies, we should think about how these facts have, for the most part, translated to a younger audience. What is their perspective and understanding of veganism and health?

Firstly, heart disease is the number one killer across the globe because high meat, dairy, and egg consumption is creating such a mess clogging up our arteries and hearts to the point of no return. Our love for animal products is literally killing us, in the millions, and accounts for billions of pounds, dollars, and Euros being spent globally on trying to band aid the issue instead of looking at the root causes. In 2019, the World Health Organisation recorded that, "17.9 million people die each year from CVDs, an estimated 31% of all deaths worldwide,"[33] which is an outrageous number, especially when they could potentially be avoided. Children can easily understand what happens when a heart attack strikes, and they can just as easily digest what caused it. Vegan children will be aware of the connection between animal fats, animal proteins, and disease. From my experience, that is really as much as they need to know.

Adults who are set in their ways and have lived a certain lifestyle for many years may have a more difficult time making that connection and may feel initially daunted by the thought of a transition to veganism. In their, maybe your, Western way of life, it is considered so much the "norm" to eat those foods because everybody else does, but it is because of those eating habits that, unbelievably in our society, tablet popping, heart attacks, and triple heart bypasses have also become the norm too. Children won't have the habits of a lifetime to grapple with; they just get it and get on with it.

> "The beef industry has contributed to more American deaths than all the wars of this century, all natural disasters, and all automobile accidents combined. If beef is your idea of 'real food for real people' you'd better live real close to a real good hospital."[34]

Secondly, humans are biologically herbivorous and are only omnivorous by choice. This is something you'll often hear vegan children talk about. It's a popular topic as they have only ever used the words herbivore and carnivore previously when referring to dinosaurs – and all children love dinosaurs. We have no instinctual urge to chase prey; we don't have claws or sharp canines that could rip the skin off of flesh. Humans have the ability to grind our teeth, ideal for eating plants, instead of the old carnivorous tear, toss, and swallow techniques of an animal who can't grind. We humans sweat through our pores instead of panting like carnivores do and, additionally, if we were obligate carnivores, our long intestines would be much shorter like those of a natural born carnivore, but they aren't, so, yeah you guessed it... herbivore.

Dr. Milton Mills stated in his presentation, *Are Humans Designed to Eat Meat?*: "In conclusion, we see that human beings have the gastrointestinal tract structure of a "committed" herbivore. Humankind does not show the mixed structural features one expects and finds in anatomical omnivores such as bears and raccoons. Thus, from comparing the gastrointestinal tract of humans to that of carnivores, herbivores, and omnivores, we must conclude that for humans it is designed for a purely plant-food diet."[35]

When it was a matter of life or death, it is no wonder that our forbearers chose to mimic carnivores and occasionally ate animals, especially when they created tools and fire for the first time and could consume their flesh more easily. Realistically though, early humans ate very little animal flesh and, as hunter-gatherers, much preferred the varieties of fruits, berries, and vegetables that they encountered on their journeys, as explained by Yuval Noah Harari in his exceptional book *Sapiens*: "It was only 400,000 years ago that several species of man began to hunt large game on a regular basis, and only in the last 100,000 years – with the rise of the Homo Sapiens – that man jumped to the top of the food chain."[36]

In evolutionary terms that is not a particularly long time, nowhere near long enough of a period of time for our herbivorous bodies to adapt to a modern, meat heavy diet. According to William Roberts:[37] "Human beings are not natural carnivores. When we kill animals to eat them, they end up killing us because their flesh, which contains cholesterol and saturated fat, was never intended for human beings, who are natural herbivores."

Thirdly, most children know, and are aware of, which foods are considered healthy from a young age. It's usually taught through sugar avoidance techniques at school, but for the most part they can confidently tell you about having five fruits or veggies a day. And let's not forget, there are enough healthy vegans including some of the world's top athletes such as, tennis player Venus Williams, Formula 1 racing driver Lewis Hamilton, footballer Jermain Defoe, boxer David Haye, snowboarder Hannah Teter, weightlifter Kendrick Yahcob Farris, mixed martial artist Nate Diaz, and pairs skater Meagan Duhamel who are living proof that humans can survive and thrive on a plant-based diet. These and many other athletes are featured in a new movie named Game Changers which goes a long way in debunking the myths about meat and changing attitudes regarding protein and strength. Children look up to these role models with awe and can plainly see what they are capable of.

The first topic within this chapter regarding animal rights is rather emotive and can make a child feel instantly sad if they are thinking about how animals are used. However, when it comes to health, children tend to feel more confused than anything else. The vegan child and their peers will all understand that eating fruit and vegetables is healthier; after all, we promote this a lot within our schools. They may not be able to truly fathom the medical intricacies of the dangers of a highly processed, high cholesterol, and high saturated, animal protein diet, but what they will know and question is, "If we don't need to eat animals for our health, and when we do so it makes us poorly, then why are we doing it?" This is central to the vegan viewpoint. If we don't need to eat animals, and it's not even healthy for us, how can we justify continuing to do it given the harm that it causes to many? And it is that thought process that you should be aware of within the classroom, especially when you are teaching about food and nutrition in science or cooking lessons.

You may find vegan children using quotes such as, "My body is a temple" or "My body is not a graveyard." If this was a key reason for your vegan child to be on a plant-based diet, you should find ways to include plant-based vocabulary and ingredients into your classroom and exclude animal-based products as much as possible or at the very least ensure that there is always a vegan option as an alternative. Many people may have also switched to a plant-based diet after a health scare and so it may be a sensitive subject, thus further highlighting the need for your full understanding. I will provide hints, tips, and recipes in Chapter 2 on how to best achieve this plant-based classroom ethos.

Finally, one topic that can't be ignored is the problem of child obesity within our schools, as 7% of children leave UK schools obese. According to the House of Commons Library, in 2018:[38]

> "9.6% of reception age children (age 4-5) are obese, with a further 13.0% overweight. These proportions are higher among year 6 children (age 10-11), with 20.0% being obese and 14.3% overweight."

It has been shown over and over again that eating a whole food, plant-based diet can initiate weight loss. Other benefits to a plant-based diet are quite remarkable too. Here's the science from the Cleveland Clinic:[39]

> "Michael Macknin led a study of obese children who were divided into two groups, and either fed a low-fat, no-oil vegan diet, or the American Heart Association recommended diet. Both groups lost weight. The kids eating the vegan diet, however, also showed significant improvements in systolic blood pressure, body mass index, total cholesterol, total low-density lipoprotein (LDL, long referred to as 'bad cholesterol'), c-reactive protein (another marker of inflammation), and insulin levels, compared to their baseline."

We know that fruits, vegetables, grains, nuts, legumes, and seeds are healthy for us. They're called "superfoods," and more often than not, cost more than processed, meaty foods, especially if they're organic. For a vegan child, it will be a little mindboggling that people eating the average Western diet will worry about the health of vegans when these children gladly choose to eat a rainbow of pure goodness from rich soil, kissed by the sun, and grown with love. Plant-based whole foods are nutrient dense with vitamins, amino acids, and minerals, and naturally rich with protein, calcium, and iron. Plus, there are thousands of species of edible plants out there. The goodness in their food hasn't been filtered through or come out of another body – dead or alive. There are no slaughterhouses or diseases involved, no antibiotics, no high saturated fats, and no frightening diseases such as Bovine Spongiform Encephalopathy (BSE), Campylobacter, E-Coli, or Salmonella. By promoting a whole foods, plant-based diet in your classroom, not only will the vegan child in your class feel more included and accepted, but you will also be benefiting the whole class by encouraging great health.

Environment

> "The wandering bands of storytelling Sapiens were the most important and destructive force the animal kingdom had ever produced."
>
> –Yuval Noah Harari [40]

Looking back at the Vegan Society's definition of Veganism, "…. promotes the development and use of animal-free alternatives for the benefit of humans, animals and the **environment**," we will now look at another fundamental reason why a family or child may choose to become vegan.

In 2006, a damning conclusion was reported by the Food and Agriculture Organisation (FAO) of the United Nations that the livestock industry at that time was, "One of the top two or three most significant contributors to the most serious environmental problems, at every scale from local to global."[41] Since then, a United Nations Environment Programme (UNEP) report,[42] released in 2010, makes for very frightening reading, but its facts are widely unknown. One of the most significant statements is that, "Agricultural production accounts for a staggering 70% of the global freshwater consumption, 38% of the total land use, and 14% of the world's greenhouse gas emissions." The report then continued to suggest, "We must start looking into our everyday activities if we truly want a green economy – for developed and developing countries." More recently, in 2017 the UNEP released a report[43] that explains how animal agriculture continues to be one of the top three highest contributors responsible for global climate change, now even more so than the collective universal transport industry. That is all of the cars, planes, trains, trucks, tractors, motorcycles, helicopters, cruise and cargo ships all put together, and is only exceeded by the energy industry.

In order to provide a little more perspective on these UNEP reports, I will spend a little time dissecting and explaining the negative effects that the animal agricultural business has on our global water and land resources, as well as expanding on the emissions issue too.

Starting with the latter, it is estimated that around 65% of all nitrous-oxide emissions are caused by raising livestock for food. For those of you who are unsure, nitrous oxide is a greenhouse gas that creates around 300 times more climate damage than carbon dioxide. Scientifically speaking, "nitrous oxide (N2O) has a GWP 265–298 times that of CO2 for a 100-year timescale."[44] The global emissions of methane and nitrous oxide are predominantly due to animal agricultural activities; methane from cows and nitrous oxide from fertilisers. As cows can produce up to 150 billion gallons of methane per day, it is easy to see how the annual output of both nitrous oxide and methane equates to a higher output than the combined travel industries.

Thus it is quite clear how our daily eating habits are impacting on future generations.

In spite of these damning figures, emissions from the animal agricultural industry are projected to increase drastically over the coming years due to demand. "The most complete published projections at the time of writing (FAO, 2006) suggest that in 2050, 2.3 times as much poultry meat and between 1.4 and 1.8 times as much of other livestock products will be consumed as in 2010."[45] If we continue the way that we are going as a species, our planet will not be able to repair the damage done. Perhaps signs that you see at Extinction Rebellion's climate change protests with a plea for people to "Go Vegan" will make more sense now.

And to the subject of freshwater, which will soon become one of our most sought after luxuries, not just in the third world, but globally. We currently use it frivolously to support the growth of billions and billions and billions of livestock where PETA[46] calculates a phenomenal 2,400 gallons of water is used to produce just 1 pound of meat in comparison to, only 25 gallons of water are required to grow 1 pound of wheat.

Almost one-fifth of the world's population face water shortages, yet a study ran by the UNESCO- IHE Institute for water education[47] showed in 2010 that, "The average water footprint per calorie for beef is twenty times larger than for cereals and starchy roots. When we look at the water requirements for protein, we find that the water footprint per gram of protein for milk, eggs and chicken meat is about 1.5 times larger than for pulses. For beef, the water footprint per gram of protein is 6 times larger than for pulses." The study then goes on to conclude that from a freshwater resource perspective, "It is more efficient to obtain calories, protein and fat through crop products than animal products." It is criminal that anyone on our planet is deprived of clean and fresh water but it is easy to see where it is all going.

Waste is another enormous environmental hazard for our already existing freshwater, and by waste I mean the excrement, urine, blood, and excess body parts collected by and disposed of by the animal agricultural industry. "Thick, black smelly tarry stuff flowing down our stream," said one resident from Sussex to the Bureau of Investigative Journalism in 2015.[48] "It was chugging along, killing little frogs, fish and invertebrates. They were wiped out," she concluded. Within this same article it was reported, "Agricultural pollution is an 'endemic problem' that is the major cause of the drastic decline in UK freshwater fish species." Unfortunately these polluting incidents are more common that you'd think with The Guardian newspaper reporting that, "Serious pollution incidents in the UK from livestock farms are now a weekly occurrence, leading to damage to wildlife, fish, farmed livestock and air and water pollution."[49] If this is happening in an idyllic setting in part of modern, rural England imagine what is happening in parts of the world with zero regulations that will be dumping their waste without ever having been held to account.

And it is not just our local waters and rivers that are affected by the animal agricultural industry. Industrial fishing is literally emptying our oceans. It is estimated that 90% of the world's fisheries are exploited or depleted and industrial fishing continues to catch more fish than is biologically sustainable. There is no replenishing, just dwindling numbers of almost every aquatic dweller. In fact, to feel the magnitude of how many species are disappearing, I urge you to type the word "overfished" into the "find" pane whilst looking at an online copy of The State of World Fisheries and Aquaculture (2018) document.[50] It is astonishing!

In addition, not only are the sea animals used for food at risk of extinction but there is also a great threat to other ocean inhabitants. The World Wildlife Fund (WWF) highlights the accidental deaths induced by the fishing trade:[51]

"In total, 38 million tonnes of sea creatures are unintentionally caught. That is 40% of fish catch worldwide. A large amount of this is either thrown back into the sea as 'rubbish,' dead, dying, or seriously injured, or disposed of on land. For some species, it is even more: for 1 kilo of shrimp, 5-20 kilos of by-catch can be found in the nets!"

Some of our most treasured and already endangered marine animals such as some dolphins, sharks, and turtles are among the waste that will no doubt, along with most fish, become extinct within a decade if this continues. This coupled with discarded ghost nets and dead zones created by the deoxygenation of our oceans due to global climate change, which is a direct consequence of animal agriculture, leaves very little hope for our marine animals or reefs.

Speaking of extinction, "Producing protein from chickens requires three times as much land as producing protein from soybeans. Pork requires nine times as much land and beef 32 times."[52] As vast lands are cleared for animals to graze on, or for their food such as soy and corn to be grown on, indigenous wildlife within those habitats are losing out. Land is usually set on fire to be cleared with catastrophic results for the immediate wildlife and wider environment. Herbivores are losing plants, predators are losing prey, and as a consequence whole ecosystems are collapsing. It is estimated that rainforest deforestation is causing the loss of 137 plant, insect, and animal species daily—an average of 50,000 species each year.[53] G. Eshel, a geophysicist at Bard College in Annandale-On-Hudson, New York, who studies how human diets affect the environment states, "Now we can say, only slightly fancifully: You eat a steak, you kill a lemur in Madagascar. You eat a chicken, you kill an Amazonian parrot."[54] We are currently witnessing the sixth mass extinction on this planet and that is wholly heartbreaking. This is a particularly hard pill to swallow if you are vegan for the environment, especially when there are so many delicious plant-based alternatives available which use far fewer resources.

Perhaps the rainforest and the species who are dying within them are far from where you live and you cannot directly see or feel the effects of the destruction there, but here in the UK there are just as many issues. The Labour Party Shadow Cabinet's 2018, environment document explains the situation regarding destruction of the environment in the UK:[55]

> "We are facing a natural environment crisis, and time is running out to fix it. Our soils are hugely depleted, with soil degradation in England and Wales costing £1.2 billion per year. Only 14% of our rivers are in good ecological condition and 63% of sensitive habitats are threatened by air pollution. Farmland bird numbers have declined by 56% since 1970, and pollinators, said to add £600 million to the value of crops each year are struggling. At least 97% of wildflower meadows have been lost. Agriculture accounts for a tenth of all UK greenhouse emissions and analysis from Defra shows little change in emissions over the past 14 years."

As mentioned previously, my veganism was first and foremost an animal rights issue, however after reading the facts listed above, I fully understand why a family or child would choose to become vegan for environmental reasons. They are quite startling. The United Nations wants us to look at our, "...every day activities" so let's do just that. What would happen to the planet if you should you cut meat, dairy, fish, and eggs from your daily habits? We know what would happen if the bees disappeared, but I wondered what difference my own choice to become vegan has made. I stumbled across the daily calculator from cowspiracy.com/facts,[56] and I was able to calculate that in the short, almost five years that I have been vegan I have saved:

1. Gallons of water: 2,007,500
2. Pounds of grain: 73,000
3. Square feet of forest: 54,750
4. Animal lives: 1,825
5. Pounds of carbon dioxide: 36,500

My daughter is currently five years old and therefore has roughly saved the same amount. That's quite a phenomenal number.

The vegan children in your class are not just the future but they are also our present. They can see the devastating mistakes that the generations preceding them have made and can foresee what the future looks like if they don't act. They are witnessing how short-sighted the generations before them have been in putting gluttony before responsibility and greed before need. I read an article recently with the headline, "Moooove Over Milk... Millennials Are Done With Dairy."[57] How humbling that the younger generation is able to hear the cries of Mother Earth and fully understand that the way the majority are living today is wholly unsustainable for future generations.

The state of the Earth is not your fault, you didn't cause it. The responsibility lies fully in the politics and corporations who created the supply and demand chain that allowed these things to go on for so long. Having said that, if the vegan child in your class is vegan for the environment and wishes for environmental issues to be discussed at your school, you should nurture them, encourage discussion, and support all that they are striving for. They may even influence you to take additional positive individual steps to help our desperate environment. After all, we will only ever have two true homes, our body and our planet, and as covered in this chapter and the last, they are both equally as precious and at terrible risk.

Compassion

"Don't talk about peace and love when you have a dead animal
on your plate."

–Socrates

Another huge misconception is that vegans believe they are superior to everyone else and that is why they "force their views"
on others, or that they only care about animals' rights and not
humans' rights. Having looked again at the Vegan Society's definition of veganism, it is quite clear that vegans do not feel that
they are better, superior, or more intelligent than anyone else; in
fact, it's quite the opposite. Vegans see all sentient beings as equal
from the human – to the ant, to the giraffe, to the mouse, to the
whale, to the crab, and all in-between. Vegans promote veganism
for many different reasons and encourage others to do the same
with social justice for all in mind; we tend to be empaths and do
not discriminate against any species. Over the millennia where
religion or nationalism may have failed to unite and have instead
caused wars or discontent, veganism tries to counter this and
promotes working towards a common purpose which is unity
and respect for Earth and all Earthlings.

Remember the Vegan Society definition of Veganism, how
it "....promotes the development and use of animal-free alternatives for the benefit of **humans**, animals and the environment."
How marvellous that the vegan child in your class has maintained their innate compassion and embraced a deeper respect
for the people, animals, and nature around them at such a young
age. They deserve their teachers and their school to become more
vegan-inclusive and it starts here, right now, with you.

Within this subheading, I will outline ways in which
humans, as well as the animals, are abused, mistreated, and negatively impacted by animal agriculture. This may open a few
windows in to the industry that you may have been completely

unaware of until now but, as far as compassion is concerned, the further we can extend this, the better we will become as a species.

Firstly, we will take a look at the third world countries on our planet and more specifically world hunger. As a teacher, I love a good visual. Check this out from PETA UK.[58]

EARTH'S HUMAN POPULATION 7,383,894,000+

THE NUMBER OF PEOPLE THAT COULD BE FED WITH FOOD CONSUMED BY CATTLE 8,700,000,000+

In other words, according to Dawn Moncrief of *A Well-Fed World*, "If we reduced our meat consumption, there would be more than enough food and other resources to be used to fill that gap and even do much more than fill that gap to make food resources available to the poorest of the poor. They are the ones getting crunched with the biofuels, but again it's just a drop in the bucket compared to what we could be doing if we reduced meat consumption."[59]

The West is growing and importing grain from Third World countries to feed the "livestock" that they in turn will eat, leaving those countries with an insufficient amount of food to feed their own population. You may be familiar with the potato famine in Ireland of 1845. A BBC article from Jim Donnelly entitled the "Irish Famine" draws a, "food gap" comparison:[60]

"There existed — after 1847, at least — an absolute sufficiency of food that could have prevented
mass starvation, if it had been properly distributed
so as to reach the smallholders and labourers of the
west and the south of Ireland. Why, then, was an
artificial famine permitted to occur after 1847, and
why didn't the British government do much more
to mitigate the effects of the enormous initial food
gap of 1846-47?"

Nowhere in this modern day and age should there be a
starving population and especially not, when in other parts of
the world, there are growing obesity crises. The current governments and animal agricultural industries are deliberately
causing this disparity in weight and health for monetary gains,
just as they did in the 1800's in Ireland and the 80's in Ethiopia.
Vegans, and more specifically the vegan child in your class, will
choose not to support this by asking the same question asked
by Jim Donnelly, which is obviously "why isn't the government
doing more?" And whilst holding governments responsible and
demanding change, vegans will simultaneously decline to support animal agricultural industries by abstaining from buying
their products; after all, it is greed that ultimately keeps this
disparity in full force. Most vegans will choose to buy products
from local, ethical and eco-conscious companies which you
should try to consider when perhaps buying products for your
classroom. Products that may for example contain palm oil or
have been made in a sweatshop factory may very well be vegan
as they don't contain animal products but the wider issues and
ramifications are vegan issues such as exploitation and habitat
destruction. You may have heard the phrase which describes
this act beautifully said by sustainable food advocate and author Anna Lappé, "Every time you spend money, you're casting
a vote for the kind of world you want."[61]

Another way in which animal agriculture impacts negatively on the lives of people is with regards to the conditions workers within the industry find themselves in. Two excerpts from The Guardian,[62] 2018, shine a light on the appalling conditions:

> "Earlier this year, the Health and Safety Executive said the slaughter industry was at the 'top end' of its 'concern level' for injury rates. Its study found that in six years, 800 UK abattoir workers suffered serious injuries, 78 required amputations and four died while at work."

As well as these injury concerns, workers in slaughterhouses are documented as being psychologically affected, perhaps even more than physically. Slaughterhouse workers are more likely to suffer from posttraumatic stress disorder, perpetration-induced traumatic stress, and develop high instances of violence and stress-induced alcohol and drug abuse. These workers are paid the absolute minimum wage possible, work long hours, and are often seen as the "bad guys" despite their despair in a profession which pays them little respect and little wages, whilst lining the pockets of the multi-billionaires who run the show. I have posted a link to the full article in Resources, which makes for jaw dropping reading. The point that I found most harrowing was in reference to the type of workers who labour there.

> "EU migrants make up 69% of Britain's meat processing workforce – and unions believe this means many have little knowledge of their rights or how to complain. A study by the Gangmasters and Labour Abuse Authority warned that criminal groups were trafficking foreign nationals to the UK to provide labour for the slaughter racket."

It's incredibly sad to say, but within the slaughterhouse every individual, man or animal, is treated as a commodity, with next to no value or worth. Furthermore, there are many people around the world who live in close proximity to slaughterhouses and suffer from health issues as a direct result of the toxic waste prevalent in the animal agricultural business. You can imagine how much waste is created en masse when considering the sizeable amount of animals killed per hour. Forgetting for a second the bone, skin, and offal waste each animal will produce upon slaughter, they each will have also urinated, excreted, and been bled dry whilst on site too. It all has to go somewhere and as previously mentioned not only is it seeping into waterways but is also expelled by air causing health issues and additional stress due to property value decreases.

Whichever reason your vegan child initially chose to go down the vegan path, all of the above reasons soon merge into one profound ideology that umbrellas the lifestyle. It is far from being "just a diet"; it is compassion in its rawest form. Becoming vegan immediately changes your perspective on life and has a positive impact on the world around you in immeasurable ways. However, becoming vegan can be just as daunting as it can be exhilarating. You are no longer contributing as much to the suffering of animals, people, and the planet, but you have to experience the mental anguish of living in a world full of contradictory actions seen as "the norm" by most.

Vegan Psychologist and Communications Trainer Dr. Clare Mann uses the word "vystopia" to describe the existential crisis experienced by vegans in her book called *Vystopia, The Anguish of Being Vegan in A Non-Vegan World* to assist vegans who feel overwhelmed.[19]

By eliminating all, or at the very least most, of the reminders of why a child chose to go vegan from your classroom practice, you are eliminating the chances of them becoming upset at the wrong time. A vegan-inclusive classroom will be a sanctuary where those negative thoughts about animal abuse, planetary destruction, or health worries can be put to one side and the learning can take precedence.

My hope is that this chapter will have brought to light for you some of the key issues that a vegan child has to think about and contend with each day. These topics by and large are quite dark, based on torture, murder, and exploitation, which even an adult would find quite difficult to deal with. Currently, and at many times throughout the day, your vegan child will be reminded of the facts above and will somehow have to deal with them whilst trying to also juggle their spelling, grammar, punctuation, and mental maths. The vegan child will go home and ask questions along the lines of, "Why does my best friend drink the milk from cows when it means newborn calves have to die?" which has happened to me with my own daughter. It is difficult to answer, knowing that her best friend is a very sweet girl who is genuinely and blissfully unaware of these practices. They know the truth and, although it is sometimes confusing, at least they are making life choices based on reality. The vegan child will always be questioning those around them, "Why are they different?" "Do they know what is going on and are choosing to ignore it?" "What do they eat?" "What do they wear?" As much as I welcome discussions and debates surrounding vegan topics and could personally talk on this matter all day long I appreciate that you have a wide syllabus to deliver and not enough time as it is. Therefore, to be as effective as possible keep reminding yourself that it is your job as an inclusive and caring teacher to simply remove as many of the negative triggers as possible so that the vegan child can concentrate on their learning and socialising at school.

Going forward, you now have a sense of what it means to be vegan. Furthermore, you understand that vegans see the world from a different perspective than their non-vegan peers. In addition, you can recognise that special provisions should be implemented in order to help the vegan child, or children, in your class feel included and valued. Those were the aims of Chapter 1, and now Chapter 2 will show you how.

How Can You Make your Environment More Inclusive for Vegan Children?

~~~~~~

As an inclusive teacher, you are probably starting to think about the issues laid out in Chapter 1 and potentially questioning whether or not the vegans have a point. All children are constantly trying to make sense of the world around them as they grow, which can sometimes be overwhelming. Not only do vegan children have to deal with the anguish of knowing what is happening to billions of their furry, feathered, and finned best friends, but they also have to live in a world where most of the people around them think that it's okay for things to be this way. It is important that they know the truth and make informed decisions. As I said in the Introduction, I wished that I had learned about animal agriculture sooner, but those truths can also be burdensome. Children are new to the world and for the vegan child it is an even more surreal world, resonant of Lewis Carroll's world where Alice stated, "It would be so nice if something made sense for a change."[63] Their minds are already blown and now you have to demand their concentration in order to teach them their ABCs or perhaps a Shakespearean sonnet. This chapter outlines some of the things that you can do to enable the vegan child in your class to forget about those issues and temporarily concentrate solely on their learning.

Curriculum Planning

"I propose that restoration be made part of the educational agenda. Every public school, college and university is within easy reach of streams, rivers and lakes that are in need of restoration. The act of restoration is an opportunity to move education beyond the classroom and laboratory to the outdoors, from theory to application and from indifference to healing. My proposal is for institutions to adopt streams or entire watersheds and make their full health an educational objective."

–David W. Orr[64]

At this point, I think that it would be useful to provide some vegan-inclusive topic plans to assist in replacing topics that you may have planned on teaching but now realise aren't vegan-inclusive and wish to replace. The vegan-inclusive topic plans provided are animal centred yet vegan-friendly, as they are based on animals in their natural habitats. These vegan-inclusive topic plans show you how you can still use animals to teach key skills, but they skip the parts where animals are exploited. You can edit, swap, change, or add to all of these vegan-inclusive topic plans as you teach them and as your knowledge increases each year you'll become more confident, comfortable and creative. You may already own plans for habitats such as the rainforest or the ocean. It's perfectly fine to teach those topics, but now that you are taking into consideration the vegan child's viewpoint, perhaps you could replace the zoo or aquarium trips and keep the rest. If you have been teaching the same topics for many years, you may even enjoy the chance to enhance and improve what may have become repetitive.

Children should be taught to understand the world they live in, to have respect for the animals and plants with whom they share the Earth, and appreciate the vital ecosystems that rely on our understanding, compassion and protection.

The Pond

My first recommendation for a topic based on a natural habitat is that of the pond. In the UK, we are lucky to have many ponds to visit for a real life learning experience. When visiting ponds, it is crucial that children are fully aware that they are going to observe but not disturb the habitat in any way, either by interfering with the landscape or removing any of the living organisms, especially frogs. Thorough risk assessments will also have to be completed for the safety of both the children and pond life.

THE POND / FROG LIFE / POND LIFE / TOADS

Science – *Classifying*	**Science –** *Water*	**Science –** *Life Cycle*	**Science –** *Pond plants*	**Science –** *Evolution*
Classifying animals and understanding why the features of a frog or toad make them amphibians.	What is a pond? Looking at the pond ecosystem as a whole. Looking at its inhabitants and their interdependence on one another.	*Oscar and The Frog* The life cycle of the frog is a fascinating topic with plenty of resources readily available online.	Discover reeds and lily plants. Their function as well as their beauty can be discussed.	How are frogs able to live in a rainforest and a desert?
Literacy – *Writing*	**Literacy –** *Information Texts*	**Literacy –** *Classic Texts*	**Literacy –** *Research & Debate*	**Literacy –** *Rhyming Patterns*
Princess and the Frog This story features a frog as the main character. Discussions and lessons can be cantered around their characteristics and how frogs behave. Frogs as hunters/survival on the pond/ Calm as we think?	Create a frog information text using various research techniques and presentation techniques.	*Toad of Toad Hall* *The Wind in the Willows*	Importance of frogs in the ecosystem. Food chains A serious question could be posed on what would happen if frogs disappeared? How important are they in the food chain that extends further than the pond?	*Oi Frog* Rhyming book can be used as a way to hook younger children onto the pond topic. Children could extend their learning by writing their own poems about frogs.

THE POND / FROG LIFE / POND LIFE / TOADS				
Numeracy – *Measuring, Counting, & Calendar*	**Numeracy –** *Symmetry & Times Tables*	**Geography –** *Habitats*	**Geography –** *Human Impact*	**Geography –** *Global*
Pond depth could be calculated in a measuring lesson. Counting tadpoles could be used to practise counting up to any number. Months, seasons, and cycles can be practised when looking at the life cycle of a frog.	Are frogs symmetrical? Leapfrog counting in 2's, 5's, 10's, or more.	Look at and discover microhabitats around school. These may range from large puddles to ponds. What makes it a microhabitat?	Are pond habitats threatened?	Discover pond habitats around the world. Cultural references and comparisons can be made regarding who lives, thrives, and survives in ponds around the world.

THE POND / FROG LIFE / POND LIFE / TOADS

Art – *Watercolour*	Art – *Clay*	Design & Technology – *Construction*	Information & Communication Technology – *Research*	Information & Communication Technology – *Creative*
Claude Monet Watercolour lessons based on children learning from and being inspired by Monet's lily pad painting.	Clay models of frogs.	Design and build a pond at your school. You could fundraise beforehand to fund the project.	Research the difference between a frog and a toad. PowerPoint	Film the frogs at your pond and narrate over it. Do this over a period of time to show the difference in seasons. GoPro under the pond video.

Music – *Composition*	Religious Education – *Judaism*	Physical Education	Personal, Social, & Health Education	School Trips
Using various instruments or voices children practise pond related songs and noises. *Paul McCartney and The Frog Chorus – We All Stand Together* Kermit the Frog	10 Plagues in the Jewish Passover story. How would a plague of frogs affect the land, people, and wildlife?	Children replicate frogs as jumpers and climbers. Leapfrogs game can be played in teams.	Totem Animal Spirit as Symbol of transformation.	Regular visits to a pond, see spawn, then tadpoles, then frogs.

Without a doubt, this topic is one which will keep children engaged and imaginative. The pond is a habitat that the children can visit often, especially if there is one nearby or built at school. Thankfully there are hundreds of children's books on this topic too, including *Jump, Frog, Jump!; In the Small, Small Pond;, An Extraordinary Egg; Pond Walk; and Life in the Pond.*

Recently, I visited a school that had no access to a pond, so we researched who would be most likely to live in a pond, practiced drawing them, and found out facts about them such as what they ate and who ate them. Once we had all of that information, I laid out two huge blue pieces of sugar paper and the children stuck their own pond inhabitants and plants onto it. We hung in onto the wall after we had finished and were able to enjoy our very own ecosystem in the class.

The Forest
The next topic plan recommendation is based on the forest, woodlands, or any small area where trees have gathered and grown. This will suffice so long as there is life within those trees using them as their home and habitat. Whether a forest or woodland, this topic is a great one for imaginations and explorations.

THE WOODLANDS/ FOREST

Literacy – *Reading*	Literacy – *Story Writing*	Literacy – *Poetry*	Literacy Design, & Technology – *Instructions*	Science – *Fair Test*
There are a tonne of stories, poems, and films which are based within a forest or woodlands and have immense literary value. Here is a selection of my favourites: *The Gruffalo; The Chronicles of Narnia; Forest has a Song; A Bug's Life; Bambi*	Story writing about animals who live in the forest can be great to show they fully understand who lives there and what a forest/woodland setting looks like. Perfect for descriptive language.	Poetry using the word FOREST as an acrostic poem.	How to build a bug hotel. Children design and create their own bug hotels, step by step.	Fair tests on how plants grow can also be conducted. Observe seeds with and without light, water, or the correct temperature.

THE WOODLANDS/ FOREST

Science – *Project Work*	Science – *Research*	Science – *Species*	Science – *Habitats*	Science – *Growing*
Visit and plan lessons within woodlands. Visit each season so that children specifically look at the changes throughout the year.	Discuss the meaning of hibernation. Who hibernates? Why? Discover the different layers within the forest canopy. Compare and/or collect different leaves and seeds from different forests around the world.	Species dependency and the parts played within the ecosystem.	Take a closer look at the insects who live in the forest and woodlands. Perhaps conduct a butterfly watch. Habitat research and fact sheets.	Growing trees to eventually plant around the school, from seeds. The earlier this is done the more benefit the child will see as they watch it grow through the years. Life span of a leaf.

THE WOODLANDS/ FOREST

Science – *Senses*	Science – *Mapwork*	Numeracy – *Counting*	Numeracy – *Measuring*	Numeracy – *Measuring*
Take the children on a nature walk. Use their five senses to record what they have perceived.	Take a look at forests or woodlands on a map. Compare older maps to newer maps. Research and compare different types of trees.	Children create shapes with twigs, leaves, and other forest finds.	Measure the growth of seeds as they grow into plants. Collecting and measuring rainfall from leaves with different spans.	Discuss shelters and how they have been used all around the world and since the dawn of tools. Build a school shelter. Measure length and height of shelter materials.

THE WOODLANDS/ FOREST

Numeracy – Counting	Numeracy – Shape	Information & Communication Technology	Music – Composition	Art
Find twigs and use them in any which way possible.	Find shapes in the forest. Draw a forest using those shapes.	Google Earth is a great tool for enabling the children to look at vast expanses of forests, especially the Amazon. Conversations could also be held regarding its destruction using chronological depletion photographs.	Making music from nature is a fun way to try and replicate some of the sounds they have heard on the nature walk. The children can use the collected items from their walk as instruments.	Children create their own nature pictures using twigs, leaves, and other forest finds. Leaf printing is also a great way to create colourful pictures.

THE WOODLANDS/ FOREST

| Art – | Art – | Art & Design – | Forest School | Physical Education |
Clay	*Artist Profile*	*Recycling*		
Clay modelling using twigs, leaves, and other forest finds.	Study an artist such as Pete Gilbert who has painted or drawn forests and children can try and emulate their work.	Trees, paper recycling Children can look at the process of how paper is made, how paper is recycled, and what sustainable practices are being used.	Arrange a trained Forest School teacher to visit your school if you are lacking in woodlands. *The Happiness Tree* is a great book written by a Forest School leader, Danny English. This book can be used as an initial hook to engage children.	Woodland workout, physical activities such as freestyle climbing.

THE WOODLANDS/ FOREST

Personal, Social, Health, & Economic Education	Religious Education & History – *Buddhism, Judaism, & Christianity*	Assembly – *Drama*	Just for Fun	History
A Tree Grows: A Listen Along Story Teaching Children The Value of Patience is a short video about patience, self-esteem, and diversity which is lovely to share with the class. Children could also create their own family tree using old photographs of family.	In Buddhism, the Bodhi tree has come to represent a number of symbols. According to Jewish mythology, in the Garden of Eden there is a tree of life. In Christianity, the "Tree of Life" is mentioned in the Bible in the *Book of Genesis*.	*The Man Who Planted Trees* is a free online resource from the Woodland Trust that provides an exciting and informative assembly to be performed.	If a tree falls in the forest and no one is there to hear see it, does it still make a sound?	Research an exciting forest such as Sherwood Forest in Nottingham that has famous kings, Queens, or heroes such as Robin Hood. Where does the term "tree hugger" come from?

You could concentrate on the whole forest, the woodlands near you, or you could specifically focus on one tree that resides on your school grounds. You could visit the tree as a class throughout the seasons, and maybe eco-decorate it when you do. You could write about imaginary fairies or pixies who live in it and focus on its microhabitats. Be thankful for it breathing, for its shelter, and for the protection that it provides, and even eat a picnic or two around it. Draw it, paint it, count its leaves, and perhaps you could name it too. These are beautiful ideas to get children out of the class and connecting with nature.

The Sanctuary

Sanctuary is one of those beautiful words that brings a smile and evokes a peaceful feeling when heard or said. My thoughts are always taken to a place of freedom, tranquillity, and peace. For children who live in a hectic home or have experienced trauma, this topic can bring solace and calm where it is much needed. The happy ending of an abused animal can bring comfort and hope to a child who themselves might be searching for one too.

I find this sort of holistic topic equally important for the children with bundles of energy as an opportunity to channel that energy to focus and discover the much underused crafts of meditation, contemplation, and reflection, even for the busiest of minds. This is a topic that delves into what it means to be free, how that feels for all living beings, and how we ourselves define freedom. With respect and compassion at its core, there are plenty of interesting discussions to be had and journeys to take, together.

Now admittedly, an animal sanctuary is not necessarily a natural habitat, but there is no denying that they are well-intentioned homes that have the animals' best interests at heart. It is because of this that I would recommend teaching about animal sanctuaries as there is a lot to be learnt about compassion, animal care, and animal rights from their existence.

THE SANCTUARY / SANCTUARY / FREEDOM				
Literacy – *Poetry*	**Literacy –** *Sequencing Events*	**Literacy –** *Recount*	**Literacy –** *Creative Planning*	**Literacy –** *Classic Texts*
Further examine the phrase "Free as a bird." Ask the children where they feel it originated from. Follow up with some bird spotting and write a poem titled "Free as a Bird," describing what they saw.	Discover experiences before, during, and after a capture. Great for initiating some deeper conversations. Animal examples could be from factory farm to sanctuary. Human examples could be from a prisoner of war camp story.	Visit an animal sanctuary. Children write a recount or an informational text of their visit.	Fundraise for the sanctuary that you have visited to show them your support. Design and implement the campaign as a class.	Nelson Mandela's *Long Walk to Freedom* is an exceptional book for older children describing both his time in prison and time as South Africa's president.

		THE SANCTUARY / SANCTUARY/ FREEDOM		
Literacy – *Letter Writing*	**Literacy –** *Comparisons*	**Literacy, Information, & Technology**	**Numeracy –** *Measurements*	**Numeracy –** *Word Problems*
Write a letter to a sanctuary thanking them for their tireless work. Also, choose a species whose home and habitat is currently threatened and write an inspirational plea to whoever is destroying it.	Take both of the letters written (sanctuary and plea) then compare and contrast the tone and language used in each. How do they differ? *Would you live on a desert Island?* Teach about the negatives such as lack of shade, food, tropical storms, etc. Perhaps compare these to positives such as peace, tranquillity, no pollution, habitat without destruction, etc.	Think back to an animal they met at the sanctuary. Children could research that animal to create an individualised passport.	Design your own sanctuary and measure correctly on the blueprints.	Create word problems to price how much it would be to run a sanctuary, e.g., how much hay for the horses, costing per bail, and how many would be necessary to feed a certain amount of horses for a certain amount of time.

THE SANCTUARY / SANCTUARY/ FREEDOM

Science – Habitat	Science – Survival	Humane Education	Humane Education	History & Geography – Comparisons
If you are lucky enough to live by one, arrange a visit to a National Marine Sanctuary.	Basic needs of survival for both animals and humans. Are these met in captivity?	Animal care in a natural environment. Discover how animals care for one another. Animal family games could be played matching the babies with their parents using photographs and language.	Collectively create a sanctuary space within the school grounds for wild animals. Perhaps this could be a hedgehog den, bird box, or a water pool for drinking. (This space will be used to encourage wildlife at the school, for observation only.)	Children discover different homes from around the world. Compare and contrast their positives and negatives. This activity can be extended to animal homes also. Animals as architects - nests, webs etc.

THE SANCTUARY / SANCTUARY/ FREEDOM

Personal, Social, & Economic Education	Personal, Social, & Economic Education	Personal, Social, & Economic Education	Personal, Social, & Economic Education	Personal, Social, & Economic Education
Should there be a place for the displaced? Older children will enjoy an immigration debate – relevant news articles can be used to discuss bias.	Freedom of speech is something that a lot of countries take for granted. Discussions can be based on, "Is this human right from birth?" *Choice* is a word that comes up a lot in vegan arguments. Ask children to think about slaughterhouses. "Our personal choice ends where someone else's choices begin."	What does it mean to be free? Used as a conversation starter this can be used for both humans and animals.	Refugees, who are they? Celebrate annual Refugee Week. This usually happens globally at the end of summer. Plenty of information can be found online. Celebrate Fairtrade Fortnight which usually happens in spring and deals with the issue of fairness at work.	Ask the children, 'What is democracy?' Develop an appreciation for democracy through various comparison lessons showing regimes that aren't democratic. Compare positives and negatives.

THE SANCTUARY / SANCTUARY/ FREEDOM

Religious Education – *Judaism & Christianity*	Religious Education – *Sacred Houses*	Art – *Drawing*	Debate	Physical Education and Music
Judaism– Noah's Ark as a symbol of sanctuary. Christianity– the stable seen as a sanctuary. Discover "moksha" also called "vimoksha," "vimukti," and "mukti," terms used in Hinduism, Buddhism, Jainism, and Sikhism which refers to various forms of emancipation, enlightenment, liberation, or release.	Take the children to visit holy houses, e.g., Gurdwara or church and compare them to regular houses to see what makes them so special. Discuss why these buildings are seen as sanctuaries.	Observational drawing or painting of animals at a sanctuary. Perhaps a sleeping pig. *Expressive art* with no boundaries. Discover Fauvism, Surrealism, and Abstract Expressionism and ask the children to emulate these freestyle art techniques.	Desert islands are sometimes seen as sanctuaries; however, scenarios could spark debate such as, "If you were stranded on a dessert Island with no food, would you eat a deceased person?" Older children could read experts from Piers Paul Read's 1974 book, *Alive: The Story of the Andes Survivors.*	Discover the South African freedom dance. This activity will be about letting go of all inhibitions and feeling free. Children can also undertake lessons in Yoga and Meditation throughout the topic. Explore different types of movements and music that create a feeling of freedom. "The Specials"–*Free Nelson Mandela* song.

I have taught a very similar topic to the one above over the half term which housed Fairtrade Fortnight. With a Key Stage 2, Year 4 (ages 8 - 9) class, we used the book *Journey to Jo'burg* by Beverley Naidoo as the hook to learn about the hardships faced by people in developing countries. This topic would be the perfect opportunity to discuss animals and their freedoms too, as listed above, which would evoke some thoughtful conversations, especially in an upper Key Stage 2 class (ages 9 - 11). Since teaching this topic and feeling so moved by it, I became the Fairtrade Champion in the town where I live and can only hope that it had an impact on the children to whom I taught it. This topic is emotive and, if taught properly, can help to shape the compassion of our next generation.

The Bug Hotel

Bugs are fascinating for many different reasons, be it their translucent wings, gangly legs, numerous eyes, their ability to spin a web, or craft a cocoon. In their own individual way, they contribute so much to this world despite being so tiny and for the most part hidden. Can you remember being young and seeing a wiggly worm in the mud for the first time? Was it a euphoric moment or a hysterical nightmare? The contrast in children's reactions to different insects is spectacular and well worth bringing into your classroom setting, not literally of course. Find out if the children love or loathe the spider, butterfly, millipede, stick insect, wasp, bumble bee, or hornet and show these creatures in all their glory. One thing is for sure, if this topic is taught correctly, the children will definitely grow in respect for those insects and will have learnt to appreciate their necessity and beauty, albeit from afar for a few who just can't shake the heebie jeebies.

THE BUG HOTEL

Literacy – *Classic Texts*	Literacy – *Descriptive Writing*	Literacy – *Diary Writing*	Literacy – *Poetry*	Literacy and Communication & Technology
Roald Dahl's *James and the Giant Peach* has an exciting array of insect characters.	Imagine you can fly, what can you see below?	Entry: A day in the life of a bug.	Write a Haiku poem about a butterfly or a bee.	Research insects and create a PowerPoint presentation based on findings.
Superworm by Julia Donaldson shows the worm as more than just a burrower.	Imagine you are a small bug, how do the noisy cars and big feet appear to you?	One child can write a day in the life of a spider whilst their friend could write a day in the life of a fly and see how the two perspectives might complement one another.	By allowing the children to choose their own insect it will encourage better writing.	
Rewrite *We're going on a Bear Hunt* by Michael Rosen as *We're Going on a Bug Hunt*.				

THE BUG HOTEL

Numeracy – *Multiplication*	Numeracy – *Symmetry*	Numeracy – *Charts*	Science – *Survival*	Science – *Classifying*
Count the spots on the back of a ladybird in multiples.	Decorating butterfly wings. Counting in multiples using drawings of insect's legs.	The children take part in a bug hunt and use a tally chart to record their findings. Similarities and differences could also be made into a "Top Trumps" game where children score the skills of insects.	Examine adaptation and survival mechanisms that insects possess.	Classifying insects into categories based on similar features, e.g. exoskeleton, invertebrate, etc. What makes them unique?

THE BUG HOTEL

Science – *Observations*	**Science –** *Habitats*	**Science –** *Life Cycles*	**Music**	**Music**
Natural composting somewhere on the grounds of the school will show children how wonderful worms are. (Don't buy worms, they will find their own way in!)	Together create a habitat map of your school's microhabitats. Take a look at the ecosystems in the local vicinity and create a larger map. Perhaps extend to looking at habitats and eco-systems in the country.	Explore the life cycles of various bugs. *Monkey Puzzle* by Julia Donaldson is a great book that supports this learning for younger children.	*A Bug's Life* soundtrack could be used as a hook to match different instruments to the sounds that various insects make. Perhaps the children could compose their own piece of music based o the sounds that they have created.	*Out of the Ark* has created a purchasable minibeast song book with 13 original mini-beast songs.

THE BUG HOTEL

Music and Physical Education	Art – *Artist Profile*	Art & Information Technology	Art – *Textiles*	Design & Technology
Children dance to Disney's *Ugly Bug Ball*.	Examine *The Insect Portraits of Levon Bliss*. Recreate or use insect drawings created by M.C. Escher as inspiration for their own versions.	Children design and build a large bug hotel using recycled, natural materials. Check and record who lives there using a spy camera.	Bugs made from junk modelling and natural materials discovering different textures.	Design a new insect species and build it from various materials.

THE BUG HOTEL

Information, Communication, & Technology	Information, Communication, & Technology – *Documentary*	Religious Education – *Judaism & Islam*	Physical Education	History
BEE – BOT® programmable floor robot.	*Life in the Undergrowth* is a wonderful BBC television series by Sir David Attenborough. Can children make their own?	Judaism– Look at the part insects played in the Ten Plagues. Islam– Read about Prophet Sulaiman and the Ant. With the children discover what lessons can be learnt from this story.	Ask the children to emulate the way that insects move.	Teach about insects from mythology and their importance e.g. scarab beetle in Egypt.

THE BUG HOTEL

Personal, Social, & Economic Education	Debate	Humane Education	Humane Education and Debate	Humane Education – *Growing*
Investigate dependency and communication in swarms, hives and ant hills. Could we learn anything from the insect world about cooperation and teamwork?	Pesticides are a key topic to hold a debate on. Pros versus cons and the effect on insects.	How does litter affect bug life?	Insects in the pet trade are another emotive topic. Insect mass extinction is another deep topic for discussion, especially now that many species, including the bee, are on the endangered list. Friends of the Earth *The Bee Cause* provide a lot of useful and free online information with regards to saving the bees.	Gardening around school specifically to attract insects. Planting seeds that will attract pollinators. Conversations about their importance.

National Insect Week is a great hook with which to begin this summer topic and usually happens in June. The National Insect Week's website provides loads of great resources including Instar magazine for young entomologists, learning resources, videos, competitions, and events.

I once started this topic with the question, "How come you don't see as many dead bugs on the windshield anymore?" Although their existence is in danger, and more species are being wiped out than ever before, this does not necessarily have to be the focus of the topic. Insects, minibeasts, and their lives are so different from ours and yet so alien and fascinating, each with their own amazing intricacies and skills. I'd be more inclined to create insect-based superheroes like Spiderman, but imagine if it was a ladybird or a praying mantis. How would that look? What skills or powers would you have? Could you write a comic strip using some of the new fictional characters which have been created in the classroom?

I can also fondly remember making symmetrical tissue paper and P.V.A. (polyvinyl acetate) glue colourful and translucent butterfly wings which looked superb up against the window of our classroom.

The Swamp/The Bog

The swamp or bog may be a habitat that your children have not visited as yet. They tend to have a reputation for being dangerous and rightly so in some cases. It is because of this that the bog makes a great topic, especially for those more adventurous or imaginative children. Other names for bogs include mire, quagmire, and muskeg, names which sound pretty weird and inviting all at the same time. They'll hook the children in. Just like Simba in *The Lion King*, children desire to go where the light doesn't touch and are inquisitive about areas that are cordoned off. It's in their nature to explore. If taught well, this topic can run its full course with that feeling of intrigue throughout. You could even get down and dirty in your very own homemade bog!

THE SWAMP/THE BOG

Literacy – *Instructions*	**Literacy –** *Classic Story*	**Literacy –** *Descriptive writing*	**Literacy –** *Poetry*	**Literacy –** *Descriptive Writing*	**Literacy –** *Information Text*	**Literacy –** *Story*
Children make a mud pie by writing instructions.	Use the book The Bog Baby to introduce the notion of a monster living in a swamp.		**Numeracy –** *Shape*	Design a bog/swamp monster using creative and descriptive writing and matching art.	Children research the types of plants and mosses found around swamps and present this in an information text.	*We're Going on a Bear Hunt* has a section in the middle where the characters have to wade through "thick, oozy mud."
They'll include in their instructions gross ingredients that they would find in or around a swamp.	**Literacy –** *Poetry*		Guess the 3d shape in a 'swamp' tray.			Using similar language children could write their own story or descriptive poem with a similar theme.
Literacy – *Descriptive writing*	Children can create their own rhyming Poem all about 'The Swamp' or swamp monster.				**Numeracy –** *Charts*	**Geography –** *Habitats*
Write a story based in or around a swamp using the children's imaginary bog character.					Data collect information regarding the children's favourite swamp animal and create a bar chart.	How is a swamp created?

THE SWAMP/THE BOG

Information, Communication, & Technology	Science – *Evolution*	Science – *Weather*	Critical Thinking	Physical Education
Show the children Wildlife 360: Life in the Swamp.	Research food chains, food webs, producers, consumers, decomposers, predators, and prey who all live in an around a swamp.	Investigate; do swamps require a certain type of weather to remain formed?	Set the children a task to determine whether or not a swamp land can ever be built upon? In small groups they must come up with ideas for a building project. What methods or materials would they use?	*Swamp Ball* Played like dodgeball except when you are hit, you wait in the other team's territory and stay in their swamp (gym mat). *Alligator Swamp* The first of two groups lay on their stomachs (alligators). The second group are the runners. The alligators leave their circle to chase the runners. Full instructions for both games are available online.

THE SWAMP/THE BOG

Geography & Science	Geography	Research & Geography	Sensory
Visit a swamp/wetlands and record what the children see.	Swamps around the world comparisons. Which is the largest ever recorded? How do you think the surrounding landscape and/or temperature contributed?	Children research water birds and migratory birds who use swamps for survival.	Make a swamp for the children to place small plastic toys in. Children can use imaginative play and discover using jelly and/or mud.

Music & Drama	Music	Art & Design – *Stitching*	Art – *Artist Profile*	History – *Drama*
Purchasable resource from the Stage Invaders provides a superb script and songs which will enable older, Key Stage 2 children to perform a play called *Christmas in the Swamp*.	*Bedtime at the Swamp* is a fantastic resource. Throughout the book is a small song verse that repeats itself over and over. Children can use instruments to bring this repeated pattern to life.	Using the character from the *The Bog Baby* story, children can make felt toys using stitching and stuffing. Alternatively, using synthetic wool, the children could make "Bog Baby" pom-poms.	Gustav Klimt was an Austrian symbolist painter who painted a swamp. This image could be used as inspiration for the children's own artistic creations.	Recreate tactical battles that have used marshlands such as the battle of Bosworth, which took place in 1485.

Although the Bog Baby book was written for a younger audience, there is no reason why this topic could not be used for any age. Older children who would best enjoy talking about monsters and creepy, dark subjects can use their wild imaginations to create characters, stories, and art work that will keep them thoroughly engaged. There are a good few children's books based on the swamp including *Goosebumps – The Werewolf of Fever Swamp* and *Swamp Monster*. These spooky stories can be used as hooks to base the subjects around, to guide reading sessions, and also as inspiration for exciting wall displays. Even those disinclined to write may be more willing to pick up a pencil and describe their swamp monster for you. If you're lucky, they may even use some adjectives.

You and you alone will know which of the above topics will work for the children in your setting. I have provided the most obvious ideas for what you can do with these topics so that you at least have a starting point. I would take these vegan-inclusive topics, alter them, change them, and add to them knowing which aspects and areas would make your children engage the most. The beauty of teaching is that the possibilities are endless, and you can find inspiration anywhere. Some classes with behaviour issues may prefer to calmly write an informational text via PowerPoint, while others will flourish making life-size insect models out of recycled scraps and materials. In some cases, you can happily do both. You could introduce an eco week, vegan week, nature week, ocean week, or even a healthy lifestyle week and share what you have learnt throughout the whole school. Furthermore, who knows what exciting new trips your class could end up going on, or events that you and the children could attend, now that you have had the opportunity to research your local vicinity again.

Throughout these vegan-inclusive topics, you may have also noticed some similarities in content, for example, habitats and microhabitats are featured in all of them. Let's say throughout the academic year you do three historical, cultural, or futuristic topics and the other three are animal-based, there is a lot of opportunity for you to revisit language and deepen the children's understanding of the natural world with almost half of the year spent delving into the world of habitats and natural animal kingdoms.

> "We cannot win this battle to save species and environments without forging an emotional bond between ourselves and nature as well – for we will not fight to save what we do not love."
>
> –S J Gould[65]

Language Choices

> "Three blind mice. Three blind mice.
> See how they run. See how they run.
> They all ran after the farmer's wife,
> Who cut off their tails with a carving knife.
> Did you ever see such a sight in your life,
> As three blind mice?"
>
> —Anonymous

I would imagine that the popular folk song above, Three Blind Mice, is older than both you and me put together, written at a time when humans were solely dependent on animals to assist with ploughing the crops, pulling the carriage, and providing the household with dairy, eggs, meat, and clothing materials to either use or sell. It's quite marvellous to think how humans have developed since then, especially after the industrial revolution, yet this folk song along with many others that promote animal use have survived the test of time, the most popular ones being *This Little Piggy, One, Two, Three, Four, Five, Once I Caught a Fish Alive, and Baa Baa Black Sheep, Have You Any Wool?*

It would have been a huge problem for village folk many hundreds of years ago to have had a mouse problem as food was scarce and had a short shelf life, so the foundations for this song are understandable. They did not have humane mouse traps back then and they lived at a time when individual owners killed their own individual animals for food. Killing was part of the norm; they saw violence as a necessity in life, especially seeing as how public hangings and beheadings were universally seen as both the best punishment and best entertainment around. In this more civilised and modernised society, we know that cruelty of any kind is wrong and all of these subliminal messages being sent to our children from such an early age are only going to reinforce the idea that animals are here for us and not here with us.

What if children around the world were all singing songs about being kind to animals and treating them with compassion and respect instead of torturing them? What if we reverted back to a time when animals were used to depict gods? How different might that world be?

How many lives might be saved if adult murderers were deterred from torturing animals because they were taught from an early age that we should never, ever hurt them? Many serial killers spring to mind who started their violent behaviour hurting animals such as Jeffrey Dahmer, who committed the rape, murder, and dismemberment of seventeen men and boys from 1978 to 1991. He admitted that when he was a child he used to kill animals for a hobby and even impaled a dog's head on a stick and displayed it.[66] His, and other murderers' brains, are clearly wired differently than the majority, which is why they commit these acts of violence. Just what if, as a child, they were taught to love and respect animals deeply, so much so that they avoided hurting them and consequently never got that taste for killing?

Please be mindful of the songs that you sing in your classroom as chopping off tails, selling pigs at markets, shearing sheep against their will, and using hooks to drag fish from their water habitats are not the kind of activities that your vegan child will enjoy singing about, and honestly, should the rest of the class be singing them? Stick to *Twinkle, Twinkle Little Star* or *Five Little Ducks*. Better still, make up some new ones and ask the class to help you. Be creative together.

Another area to give some extra thought to is the use of common phrases such as, "Kill two birds with one stone," "Be the guinea pig," "There's more than one way to skin a cat," "Take the bull by the horns," or "Beat a dead horse." These common phrases are as old as most of the nursery rhymes we use and are far more prevalent in our everyday lives as pretty much everyone in the UK and, probably globally, uses them or similar phrases, frequently. It doesn't take an expert to look at each one of these popular sayings and figure out that they all derived from instances of animal use and abuse. As always, you are encouraged to talk about animals within your classroom, but in a way that shows respect.

My vegan nephew recently had a swimming lesson during which he was asked to angle his arm and hand so as to replicate spearing a fish. This is the perfect example of how to cause confusion and trigger upsetting thoughts during an everyday lesson. His mother, my sister-in-law phoned me straight away to report how bizarre they had found the whole experience. Let's be honest, no one has used a spear in our part of the world for a very long time. His hand could have been a speedboat, or even an actual fish, as evolution has cleverly designed them to be as hydrodynamic as possible.

Similarly, if you say to your class, "I had the most delicious bacon butty this morning," you may not realise it may upset the vegan child. You see food, but don't forget they see a murdered pig. As a teacher, and an adult, you will have learnt how to bite your tongue in social situations and refrain from saying what is on your mind to avoid conflict. The same method may be called upon to stop or edit yourself from saying what you really think with regards to your own eating habits.

Take an example. You may have been on a rotten holiday to France recently, and if you had a French child with English as an Additional Language (EAL) in your class, you may not necessarily say that you despised your trip. You know deep down that although it may be true, for whatever reason, it might hurt the feelings of your EAL child to say so and so you put your automatic filter on to spare their feelings and instead focus on the positives. It may take a little time to adjust to and get used to leaving elements of your personal life out of the classroom; however, it will make a huge difference to the vegan child who may be uncomfortable hearing how much you enjoy a bacon sandwich. Perhaps instead, comment on the delicious orange juice that you had with your breakfast, something that tastes great, but more importantly everyone can enjoy equally.

Additionally, you may have noticed that throughout the previous chapter, I referred to animals bred en masse as "animals who are farmed" as opposed to "farm animals." I choose to do so based on an article entitled "The History of Currency." It states:

"Historians note that ancient societies discovered over time that it was often easier, and safer, to exchange goods with one another than to go to battle for them. Scholars trace such exchange back into human prehistory, 10,000 years or more ago. It's been found that humans relied on barter as money, or the direct exchange of goods and services. Examples of items bartered include anything considered of value, be it food, tools, weapons, materials, property, clothing, adornments or household wares." This same article further explains that, "The barter system evolved, and certain items, such as livestock, grains and metals, gained broader acceptance as a standard means of exchange, most likely for their easy measurability. Historical records show that as early as the 10th millennium B.C. onward, certain **domestic animals such as cattle and goats** were frequently traded among individuals and societies."[67]

Farming, as the above suggests, has only been around since the 10th millennium B.C. So, it begs the question, "What were farmed animals called before that?" The answer is simple; they were, "animals." Farming is a human construct and is unnatural for animals. A field, forest, pond, hillside, or riverside are their actual natural habitats, but you'd be hard pressed to see any typically farmed animals freely roaming in their natural habitats anywhere in the UK nowadays. Modern day humans have had since the 10th millennium B.C. to get used to domesticating and referring to these animals as "farm animals" because of the fact that they have been farmed for such a long time and it appears to have stuck, especially now that they aren't found free or feral in many places anymore. Please also note how I refer to the animals as a "who" as opposed to a "what" despite Microsoft Word's spell-check programme's insistence that this is wrong.

In addition, I highly recommend using the phrase "chooses not to" as opposed to "they're not allowed" when there is an offering if a non-vegan product at school. Each vegan is allowed to eat animal products, if they choose to. No one forcing us to be vegan and so it is important to acknowledge the free will and conscious decision-making that belongs to each individual vegan. It also stops the non-vegan children from feeling as though the vegan child is missing out on tasting anything because they are not allowed to.

On a similar note, the word "normal" is one that gets bandied about quite a lot and mostly subconsciously. If used incorrectly, it can have a particularly negative connotation for members of the vegan community. For example, my daughter and I ate at a restaurant recently. We chose that restaurant specifically because they had advertised that they had a new and exciting vegan menu on offer. They were right, and we were impressed. What stood out for me in particular was the fact that the children's menu had children's vegan dishes interspersed with the non-vegan dishes, which I had never seen before. Until that point, eating out had always been a little bit like making a mosaic out of the menu with "...a bit from here, a bit from there, none of that, but definitely some of that and absolutely no dairy please." We happened to be with my daughter's best friend and her mum who asked if her daughter could have chicken nuggets. She ordered them for her daughter, and I ordered the vegetable nugget alternative for my daughter. Upon arrival, the waiter hovered above our table with two mini plates of food, which were identical to look at, and asked the question, "Who is having the vegan nuggets?" My daughter put her hand up, pleased as punch with her selection, and then he further asked, "Who is having normal nuggets?" to which her friend put her hand up. My daughter interjected with, "Does that mean my food isn't normal?"

Misuse of the word "normal" isn't something that is new to me, but it was to my daughter. I was glad that she pulled our server up on it. As mentioned previously, I had a vegan restaurant for a while where we served at least seven different types of plant-based milk. At staff training sessions, we would discuss how to speak to non-vegan customers ensuring that they felt comfortable and welcome at our establishment when realistically this may very well be a brand new experience for them or they may have even been dragged there reluctantly. One of the main points that we covered each time that we met as a staff was how to respond to the word "normal." Because of the fact that we served so many plant-based milks, we had to know them inside and out, which ones paired well with tea, and which frothed the best, we had to be experts. Each time someone asked for a coffee or tea, I would always encourage the staff to ask, "Which milk would you like with that?" and more often than not someone who drank cow's milk would reply, "Normal milk please," in a rather perplexed way. I knew that this was a question that they would not ordinarily be asked in a mainstream restaurant but, in addition to making them feel comfortable, I also felt obliged to subtly educate. It must have been the teacher in me. The script I asked all staff to work from was, "We do not serve milk from a cow, but we do have several other tasty options available. Would you like my recommendation?" Some inquisitive or vegan curious customers would follow with a question about the dairy industry and then we could explain why we don't serve cow's milk. Other times people would, for the first time in their life, just accept that our milks too were "normal" and happily drank their drink.

The assumption that vegan food is abnormal, that animal-based products are normal, or vice versa, is a clear division in our current societal outlook. Food is food and people will always choose to eat what appeals to them but, at the end of the day, no matter how normal or abnormal one may view the other's food choices, I don't think that the word "normal" should ever be applied.

To further make my point, I was at a fully vegan wedding where the servers were dishing out the buffet and putting the word "vegan," before everything such as "vegan hotpot and vegan curry." To me, as one of a handful of vegans in the packed room, it sounded ridiculous. Everyone knew the bride was vegan and that that they were at a fully vegan wedding so please just call it "hotpot and curry." I am all for labelling correctly, so that you know the food you are eating is suitable, however, there are circumstances where being aware of how you refer to it, especially in front of children who often take things literally, is something that you should always consider. This is not only because the vegan child will feel alienated, as my daughter did during our restaurant experience, but also so that it causes less of a division between the children in the class. A simple, "here's yours" and "here's yours" is really all that's necessary without the big song and dance about who has different food. This act continues to promote inclusivity.

The differentiation between someone who eats a plant-based diet and someone who is a vegan is also worth mentioning. A person can be a plant-based eater yet still wear animal skins and attend an aquarium. Plant-based eaters usually omit all animal ingredients from their diet for health reasons alone and not for animal rights, compassion, or environmental reasons.

And finally, one last term to be aware of. A flexitarian is a person who has a primarily vegetarian diet but occasionally eats meat or fish. Usually this is done out of convenience.

Materials

Alternative (to animal-based) materials are readily available from most shops and you will find that, more often than not, they will be the cheaper option too. I still always look at the label though to be sure. If you are buying cushions or a rug for your classroom, please check the label to see it is made from synthetic materials. Watch out for feathers inside of soft furnishings and suede or leather used in fancy dress items. Something like this from Fabulous Platform Shoes[68] will be a clear indicator. If you are unsure, you can always check the label or manufacturers guide.

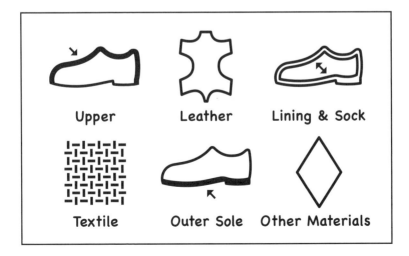

| Upper | Leather | Lining & Sock |

| Textile | Outer Sole | Other Materials |

Some glue may contain bone materials, so please always read the labels. Reading labels is something that vegan people do regularly just to be on the safe side. PVA Poly(vinyl acetate) glue is always fine.

Please take sheep's wool and silk into consideration when making soft toys or using textiles. There will always be a cheaper alternative. You may need to do a little research, but any popular search engine will be able to tell you if a product is vegan or not. When it comes to craft feathers, please ensure that ones you buy are synthetic. I have easily sourced quality products on Etsy, eBay, and Amazon.

The more natural a product is, for example wood, cork, or bamboo, the more eco- and vegan-friendly it will be. Not forgetting of course that if a vegan child became so due to environmental reasons, that biodegradable products will always be preferable, though not essential to veganism.

Another point to consider when sending home printed material is to ensure that your vegan child isn't taking home letters with summer discounts to the zoo or aquarium and such. Take a moment too when distributing dairy milk subsidy letters to think about the vegan child and parent on the other end receiving such an invitation. Sifting through letters to go home may be time consuming, but it reinforces the relationship between school and the vegan home so is well worth doing.

School Trips

At this point I wish to let you into my private life a little and talk about my recent trip to Warwick, UK. During the summer of 2018, my husband surprised our daughter and me with a weekend getaway at a hotel nearby Warwick Castle, with tickets to visit the city's castle included. Upon arrival at the castle, we meandered through a maze, learnt how to be a knight from a highly enthusiastic actor in full armour, wandered through historical displays off a great hall, booked to see the princess show later on in the day, and all the while having the most incredible historical setting and views available to us. Then we stumbled across The Birds of Prey Show, an ode to the birds of prey used throughout the medieval ages by falconers. I had noticed the show on the entrance map but chose to deliberately ignore it in the hope that it wouldn't fall onto our radar.

We finish taking photos of each other in stocks and somehow found ourselves looking directly through a tunnel with crowds cheering at the other side of it whilst the birds of prey wowed them with their stunts. We decide to go a different way and climb up an adjacent tower to get a completely different view instead. Phew. That was until our descent, when we accidently found ourselves underneath the flight path of the showpiece, namely an enormous vulture. This majestic bird was flying backwards and forwards for scraps of meat directly above our heads. We were so close at some points on the path, that we could feel the air pushed onto us by her widespread wings and truthfully, although difficult to admit, I was blown away.

The reason why I am writing about this experience, is to provide prospective on what I felt as that incredible bird flew overhead. Like you, I can appreciate how utterly jaw dropping it would be for a child to see, in real life, a tiger, a whale, or a gorilla. This was in fact the first time that I had ever seen a vulture and even me, someone who had gone out of their way to avoid this attraction, stood still taking in her magnificence along with the other hundred or so visitors. It was pure unadulterated awe. I get it. I understand why you may have wanted to take your class to aquariums and zoos. Animals are most fascinating creatures, with their evolutionary abilities, mesmerising skin colours, and species-specific sounds and nuances that make them so interesting. I can appreciate that especially for some inner-city schools, where they don't see sheep or cows on a regular basis, let alone a meercat, octopus, or giraffe, why you feel that their lives would be enriched by seeing them in the flesh.

Then the guilt crept in as I noticed the tiny cage that this giant was cooped up in upon finishing her stunt. Then I thought how unnatural it was that this vulture didn't have to hunt for her lunch, and after that, I wondered if she had ever met another vulture before. Did she like the noise of the cheering and fanfares? How much training goes into making her do this stunt? Was she ever beaten? Was she deprived of food in between shows? And then finally, was it really necessary to have her here at all when there had been so many other exciting and fun activities available that didn't involve animals?

Additionally, just think about how many of your children can tell you facts and figures about dinosaurs, which they will never see or meet. Probably more than they can tell you about an elephant and still with a sense of wonder in their eyes. You don't need to see an animal in a cage to learn about them. In this day and age, awesome technology such as 3D printing, virtual reality, holograms, and live streaming are used in everyday life. Travelling the world is more accessible and affordable than ever before, for those with a passport. We have never been more able to visit far off places both literally and technologically. The internet has everything we will ever need to know at our fingertips, and social sciences have proven that caged animals are desperately miserable, so it leads one to think, does a moment of awe mean more than freedom?

Go on trips, they're fun, and proven to create learning longevity, add value to topics, and create memories that will last a lifetime. Go to woodlands, ponds, forests and fields, rivers, beaches, and lakes. They are full of opportunities for you to teach and for the children to learn. But more importantly they are all natural habitats and the plants and animals who live there need you to value and promote these natural habitats to the next generation.

Cooking and Baking

We are extremely lucky in our household that my mum, Bernice, is also known as "The Vegan Cake Baker" and supplies beautiful cakes and bakes to restaurants in and around our town. She started baking cakes at my own restaurant and, much to the delight of our regular customers, started working full-time for herself after I sold it on. Although I am a huge advocate for the whole foods, plant-based diet, I also know that baking is a large part of the primary curriculum; it's enjoyed universally and is an important skill to learn.

My mum has perfected the vegan bakewell tart, chocolate and peanut butter cake, and sugar-free lemon loaf, amongst other delights. She uses a variety of binding ingredients which is really the only job that a chicken's egg does in a recipe. There are literally thousands of recipes on the internet which all use different binders including banana, soaked chia seeds, avocado, No Egg Replacer®, silken tofu, and applesauce. My mum uses rapeseed oil, so do I, and this is also the preferred choice for Ms Cupcake, author of The Naughtiest Vegan Cakes in Town, which I highly recommend for delicious bakes and biscuits.

At after school club, my daughter makes crispy cakes using dark chocolate, which is incredibly simple and can be found very cheaply at all major supermarkets. Just recently, her lovely teacher emailed me for a shortbread recipe. I found one which was so simple that she used it for the whole class since it only had five ingredients. Vegan baking is essentially the same as the baking that you will have been used to previously, so do not fear being creative. Use one set of vegan ingredients and instructions for all. Not only will it be easier for you to manage, but the kids won't know any different.

One helpful hint when shopping is to know that nearly all food products sold will have an ingredients list on the back and any dairy or egg items will always be highlighted in bold. I would highly recommend purchasing, at the start of each term or semester, some long-life soya milk, dairy-free margarine, and Trex® to always have on hand so you will never get caught short.

When it comes to cooking with the children, you will be required to give the recipe chosen the same amount of thought as with the baking. You will have to decide if the dish everyone will make will be vegan-friendly or will you make something animal-based for the majority, with separate ingredients for the vegan child to make their own version. If it is the latter, please be aware of the smells that might trigger upset in the vegan child. Either way, please ensure that the vegan child has their own dish to make by planning ahead and checking that you have the correct ingredients. Also, please be mindful of the fact that they may want to use their own cutlery and mixing equipment so there is no cross-contamination. I would say that it is probably less work for you if the whole class made one plant-based version together, but this is inevitably your choice to make.

Healthy Eating Displays

In a KS1 (Ages 5-6) class where I recently taught on Fridays, I planned for a science topic that was called "Healthy Eating and Exercise." Within this topic, I was expected to teach about the origins of food and how healthy or unhealthy they are. The types of food talked about as "bad foods" were mostly sugary or deep-fried foods such as sweets or chips. There was never really that grey area filled with animal fat and cholesterol. So, I taught it as it was laid out and made my point of noting that herbivores could be healthy too. Where there was a milk option, I extended it to nut milk and soya milk and where there was a butter option, I extended it to plant-based margarine. At least they know that alternatives exist. I was also able to explain that the food chain is still a food chain even if the human skipped out the rabbit and went straight to the carrot. These approaches, if used, will show your understanding of plant-based nutrition. You could also quite easily show a vegan pyramid along with your government provided, nutritional food wheel. Viva! have some wonderful information posters available on their website which I have stuck on my own fridge at home. I will add their website to the Resources section at the end. Essentially, what you are doing is providing the children with a complete overview and, by mentioning vegetarians and vegans, you are including all children and creating a sense of normality around someone's choice to eat differently. Simply ensure that you then refocus on the foods that you can all eat together and focus on our similarities for the sake of inclusion.

Another useful tool that you could implement when making healthy eating displays is instead of using fruit, vegetables, meat, and dairy as your headers on the pie chart, you could consider heading with iron, protein, calcium, minerals, and vitamins instead. This way the children can see that the body needs specific and essential nutrients and vitamins, but it does not necessarily matter which ingredient it comes from. This will also go a long way in dispelling the myth that you can't get iron, calcium, or protein from plant-based sources. Please also be aware of any changes that may occur in government provided nutrition wheels, as they do change all of the time based on new information. Canada is a perfect example; they have recently removed dairy.

I would also be aware of having pictures of meat on the wall if your class has designed a nutrition-based display, as this will most likely upset the vegan child. This also extends to plastic-shaped ones in your classroom's toy kitchen. I also encourage you to notice, especially at times such as Easter or Christmas, to count how often you see a carcass on a billboard as you drive from point A to point B. I can vouch for how difficult it is to see these images plastered all over town, so please avoid doing this in the classroom which should be a safe place.

Class Pets

This very morning, as a family, we had to have a difficult discussion about the class rabbit at my daughter's school. A permission slip came home last night asking if children were allowed to feed and stroke the rabbit; for allergy reasons they were being cautious. My husband is allergic to most animals, so this is a fair question. However, what did not feel fair was the mental journey that I then had to endure off the back of this letter coming home. "Why have they got a rabbit? Oh, that poor lonely rabbit, how sad? Why on earth have they got an animal surrounded by rowdy 5-year olds? Should my daughter play with him/her? Can she partake in feeding him/her even though we don't agree with breeding animals and keeping caged pets? She loves animals, so wants to play with him/her? Should she be included, or should she be excluded? Should we? Shouldn't we?"

What choice do I have? I can't ask our new school to get rid of him/her after having only been attending since September 2018, since it's only January 2019, and my daughter had expressed an interest in playing with him/her because she loves animals. In addition, I wasn't paying money to the breeder or for the animal to remain caged as my entrance at a zoo turnstile does; he/she is already there so if you can't beat them, join them. It pained me to think that, but it did cross my mind, which was moving at one hundred miles per hour. Am I right? Am I wrong? I doubt that there is a right or wrong answer in this case, it is after-all subjective. Would I be putting my daughter's happiness before that of an animal? Is that the vegan thing to do? And so, it went on all night and all morning until finally, and begrudgingly, I signed it, "When all said and done, it's feeding a rabbit who is already there" I thought. And it still haunts me to this day. Other vegan parents may not have signed it. This kind of anguish is real and it can be avoided by having no class pets.

I can see the perceived value in keeping a pet at school, lessons to be learned about how to clean and care for him/her, and also in providing for children, those in the inner cities especially, an opportunity to connect with an animal if they have never done so before. The pet trade though ultimately puts financial gain above what is best for the animals. Vegan children believe that breeding animals as pets is wrong, as it contributes to many problems including unwanted animals who are eventually "euthanized," and the fact of the matters is that animals should live in their natural habitats and be with their families. Just because an animal is used to the noise of the children, it does not necessarily mean that they are happy with it, especially if they are nocturnal. It is of the highest importance to consider the stress put on an animal who is passed from pillar to post each weekend, as different families sign up to look after him/her.

The cages, bowls, and hutches will always be too small and too lonely for an animal to enjoy any degree of happiness and each day they will have to dodge rough hands, screaming voices, and long for their freedom. I remember when Chinchillas were introduced into my old primary school; I mean, come on, what on earth are Andean Chinchillas doing in the middle of Cheetham Hill, Manchester?!

This same line of thought should extend to chick hatcheries at Easter, live caterpillar life-cycle displays, and wormeries. It is simply unnatural to have these fake habitats in your classroom. I cannot tell you the number of vegan parents who I have had to coach throughout spring, skyrocketing compared to any other time of the year. For vegan families it is heart breaking seeing baby chicks, warmed by the heat of a light bulb, as opposed to their own mother's warmth. Take the children outside into forests and sanctuaries, show them chicks in their natural habitats and work a little harder to create something that is actually real and more meaningful.

Empathising and seeing the world through your vegan child's eyes is a sure-fire way for you to start seeing the animals' world perspectives too. Children and animals are so similar in their needs and vulnerability.

As Ghandi[69] said, "The true measure of any society can be found in how it treats its most vulnerable members."

Cultural and Celebratory Days

One of the most common reasons expressed by people who never wish to become vegan, despite all that has been outlined in Chapter 1, is "my culture or religion simply wouldn't allow for it" or something along those lines. An Italian without meatballs, mama mia! A Frenchman without l'escargot, sacré bleu! A Jewish family without chicken soup on Sabbath, oy vey! And the list goes on.

I am reminded of a conversation that I had with my niece who is six years old and attends a Jewish School. In a passing conversation she asked me, "Why don't you eat chickens?" She further reported, "They don't feel pain when they are killed in a special way, shochet, so it is okay to eat them, my teacher told me so." I was told the same as a youngster and it is a pretty compelling story. Why wouldn't she believe her teacher? We are taught that what the teacher says is gospel and that our teachers love us. As teachers you also know this to be true. Why would her teacher lie? I would be as bold as to say that this is genuinely what her teacher truly and innocently believes, and she was probably taught that view by her own teacher. Even though this is untrue, it won't be questioned, and it is instilled as part of a belief system. To question it may undermine the respect for a teacher and perhaps undermine elements of what it means to be Jewish, or Muslim, and so the cycle continues, unquestioned.

Festivals, celebrations, and family occasions globally are almost always centred around food and eating together. Breaking bread with your neighbour, eating ritual foods on specific days, slaughtering a goat in remote villages should an important visitor arrive, wedding breakfasts, and blowing out candles on birthday cakes have been popular traditions for as long as humans have socialised. Traditions and cultures are important and should be covered in school; our differences as well as our similarities are fascinating, our history and heritage make us who we are.

On the flip side of the coin, just because something has been done for a very long time doesn't necessarily make it right. Women used to be seen as subservient and incapable of playing a part in British society, Victorian children used to be seen as workers who were exploited and man-handled, African men, women, and children were kidnapped and forced to be slaves in the West. All of these abhorrent and legal acts were seen as normal at the time, because everyone else was doing it. Thankfully social justice movements were fought and won by compassionate and determined groups – the abolitionists, the civil rights movement, the suffragettes Lord Shaftesbury, and Sir Robert Peel. Then there was reform. Times change, and as a species, we should evolve, especially with all of the improvements in faux meats, faux materials, easy access to worldwide ingredients, and plant-based creativity.

Go forth on India day at school and eat vegetable samosas. On China day, eat vegetable noodles in soy sauce. On Mexico day eat bean burritos. And on Spanish day, enjoy paella with mock chicken or mock prawns. You can even have vegan style Polish pierogi dumplings. There are thousands of recipes online to meet the need of all of your children's cultures so play music, dress up, and learn about each other. Eat, drink, and be merry. Families are still perfectly able to celebrate the traditions of their generations, together at a table, and bring that celebration to school for peers to experience, with joyous expression and delicious food. The only difference will be the lack of animal suffering.

Lunchtimes

Children will spend the majority of their school day in the same class as the peers who know them and understand them the most. Lunchtime is the only part of the day when they get to be with and see other children from around the school. If there is any bullying regarding dietary choices, it should be stamped out and addressed immediately as it would in any other bullying circumstance. Initiatives like the "Meatless Monday" may go towards creating a more understanding canteen. Even if your school does not experience these issues at all, you may want to implement a healthy "Meatless Monday" to further include your vegetarian and vegan children.

Vegan children in any formal education setting should be entitled to a plant-based option as an automatic requirement, but unfortunately this is not the case at present. I had to meet with our school, council, and catering representatives to push for my daughter to have a vegan option and even then, it had to be made elsewhere and brought in. What I have found, after doing some research, is an inconsistency up and down the country and in other countries too, with regards to which boroughs do and which boroughs don't provide plant-based options. In order to highlight what I had found, I contacted the national press to cover our story (links in Resources) and found myself in Parliament a few weeks later talking about plant-based options on all Public Sector menus, or lack thereof.

Thankfully, there are two major groups working on this who presented at that same Westminster event. The Vegan Society, with their "Catering for Everyone" campaign and Pro-Veg UK with their "School Plates" programme. Both seem to be making headway in convincing the powers that be that there should be an automatic option for plant-based meals in our schools and that there should be consistency so as to avoid vegan families being made to feel excluded. Portugal has done it, so there is no excuse for other countries not to be able to.

I was absolutely heartbroken walking around my local supermarket after dropping Lois off on her first day of school quickly gathering a packed lunch together for her to eat later in the day. Having been refused on day one and being fed the line, pardon the pun, "It's a lifestyle choice, not a religion." This made us feel so unwelcome. I cried for most of the day, a day that should have been memorable for different reasons, and considered homeschooling.

The lack of vegan food at schools that can really make a family feel excluded, it is as though they are not worth catering for and incidentally this issue is the one that I get most parents emailing me about when asking for assistance. Thankfully, when I was in that position I knew who to contact and wasn't afraid to fight for our rights; it seemed completely backwards that we were in a sense being punished for being compassionate. We have to eat; food is sustaining and it is a huge part of each day. There is the social element to sharing food, sitting together and talking about what you're eating that I didn't want my daughter to miss out on. Until plant-based options are accepted as "the norm" and implemented nationwide, it might be useful for you to know in the meantime that the Equality Act of 2010[70] supports the rights of vegan parents to ask for vegan meal options. I am so glad that I used this piece of legislation and demanded this right for my daughter to be fed along with everyone else. Thankfully now, Bury Council, the first in the U.K., has a rolling vegan menu which any parent, at any school, at any time can request and I am so proud to have been part of its implementation. Yes, the vegan child's parents could easily make a packed lunch, but the point is that for a school to say "no" they are point blank discriminating against a philosophical belief. By failing to provide vegan food upon request a school or catering company would most definitely be in breach of the Equality Act 2010. As an inclusive teacher, you may be able to help any parents unsure about asking by supporting them and showing that you agree it should be made available to them.

School Milk

My last teaching role before I became Senco was as the reception teacher in our early years foundation setting (Ages 4-6). Apart from the daily references to Old Macdonald and his make-believe farm, the hardest part for me was having to hand out cow's milk on a daily basis as part of a government subsidised scheme.

At present vegan children are not even eligible for government subsidy as stated on their website:

> "Not covered by the scheme. The following products aren't eligible for the subsidy:
> - products used as ingredients in the preparation of meals
> - milk other than from cows, goats or sheep; for example, soya or rice milk."[71]

The Publishing service at gov.uk are very clear on what they mean by "milk":

> "Definition of Milk 5.6.
> Milk under the Nursery Milk Scheme currently means whole or semi-skimmed liquid cow's milk which is heat treated but does not include milk to or from which chemicals, vitamins, flavours, or colours have been added or removed other than as a consequence of the process of heat treatment or as a consequence of the process of producing semi skimmed milk from whole milk."[72]

What this means in its broadest sense, is that there is still a long way to go when it comes to governments and schools removing dairy milk from their menus. Unlike Canada, they are still ignoring the fact that there's less call for dairy milk and ploughing subsidy money into the industry. At the very least though, there should be a dairy free option available, but, for now at least, families can opt out of the scheme so they are at least not being forced to consume it. Perhaps you, and your vegan parent, could discuss plant-based milks and potentially come up with an agreement for a weekly supply to be brought in. You may also be able to assist them in finding or creating petitions that call for plant milks to be more readily available at your school.

The School Fair

The biggest threat to comfort at the school fair will always be the meat-based BBQ. When vegans dine in mainstream restaurants other smells such as spices, herbs, wine, and desserts baking can override the meaty smell but there is absolutely no covering up what is cooking on a BBQ; it's the whole point of a BBQ. For vegan families, and staff who have become vegan for the animals, it will be a difficult experience for them to attend a school fair where there is a meat-based BBQ and other attractions such as small world animal stalls like "meet the lambs," birds of prey displays, or donkey rides.

There is never a good time for a vegan to see an animal being exploited, but it is somewhat tougher when it is happening whilst they are in the baking hot sun. The vegan family and/or staff member will be feeing quite torn leading up to the event about whether or not to even attend if those activities are to go ahead. The vegan child will have those same reservations; I have been there myself when it all becomes too much. It is yet another tough decision that vegan parents have to make, especially when they have the will and the want to get involved.

So, what can you do to encourage vegan families to attend? Arranging to have a number of stalls without animals is the easy part. There are an infinite number of games that can be played outside which a teacher could charge a few pennies for. If you type, "outdoor fair games" into a search engine, hundreds of ideas come up. The more difficult aspect is the food, as meat-based BBQs are still quite popular amongst the majority, they're easy to buy for, set up, and distribute. Should your school wish to continue with meat-based BBQs for ease, and that is understandable, please simply ensure that there are always vegan options and alternatives. Could you perhaps also cook the vegan alternatives in a different spot? Could you perhaps coordinate your BBQ stall so that it is around a corner and so the wind might not necessarily blow the smell across the whole yard? Do not be offended though if the vegan family does not attend, as for some, the BBQ smell is too much to handle. You could always ask the vegan family and/or staff member for recipes or advice so that they feel included, speaking to the child involved is also recommended in order to ascertain their favourite goodies. If you are in a school who wishes to change the school fair food to a plant-based only feast or at least predominantly, then you could either have a plant-based BBQ or choose a different theme and offer all the trimmings so people feel as though they have had a wide choice and are left satisfied. Perhaps you could alternate annually. There are plenty of compromises to be made depending on how inclusive you wish to be. The main thing to remember though is that as long as the food looks good, smells good, and tastes good then people will always buy it.

Reading Corner

You may have taught topics with animals in them for many years or you may have just inherited an unfamiliar classroom which has a library full of books that you may never have even read. With such an extensive job list of "things to do" on an hourly basis, sorting through your library may be the last thing on your mind. However, there will be benefits for you as well as the vegan child upon doing this job.

Firstly, you will find books that relate to topics which you didn't even know that you had, which could enhance your teaching. Secondly, you will be able to check if all of the books in your library are age appropriate and still relevant in the twenty-first century. Thirdly, you can sort them neatly into fiction and non-fiction or into topics and subjects for easy access and streamline those which you are likely to use more often. In the long run, this organisation will indeed benefit you and the whole class. More importantly, it will provide you with the opportunity to ask yourself questions such as, "Are my ethnic minority, members of all faiths, EAL (English as an Additional Language), SEND (Special Educational Needs and Disability), and vegan children represented in this selection of books?" If not, they should be, so it is time to remove irrelevant books and then do some classroom enrichment shopping.

Although it may seem like a laborious task, whilst looking through each of the books in your classroom reading area, see if any of them have stories or settings that may trigger negative thoughts for the vegan child. After reading Chapter 1, you will have a very good idea of the kind of books I mean. For example, replacing a book named Manuel the Matador with Gracias Amigos. For the record, I have made up both of those story book names, but I am hoping that you get the idea. The child will learn about aspects of Spain from a cultural story, except one doesn't involve a bull being tortured or bludgeoned for entertainment.

While there are many books that I could recommend to ensure that all children in your class are included, for the purpose of this guide I will stick to those written specifically for the vegan child, for those who wish to understand what a vegan is, and general stories with vegan characters.

Ruby Roth

Ruby Roth is an author-illustrator who introduces young readers to veganism as a lifestyle of compassion and action. Forewords describes her first book That's Why We Don't Eat Animals as "...a key resource for parents (and teachers) who want to talk to their children about this timely and important issue,"[73] and her second book, Vegan is Love, as "...conveying what children can do to protect animals, the environment and people across the world."[74] Her third book, V is for Vegan, uses the alphabet to engage children in the ABCs of being kind and is an excellent resource for children who are learning the alphabet.

Having read all three of these books, I can honestly say that each one is its own beautiful work of art. We see animals in their natural and unnatural habitats and are able to compare and empathise. We are invited to look at the world through the animal's eyes and begin to see them as individuals which some children may never have done before, especially if they have never lived with a pet or cared for an animal. We see animals in their family units and can start to see them as parents, with their offspring as opposed to as an inanimate object. For a child who may find it difficult to explain why they are vegan to friends, this selection of books explains it all on their level, with eye catching illustrations. Ruby Roth strongly believes that we should provide children with the truth about how their food is produced and give them more credit to make their own life choices by putting the power into their hands. As she passionately states in a superb interview (link provided in Resources), "It's never too early to begin learning how our individual choices affect the public realm."

How to Eat a Rainbow: Magical Raw Vegan Recipes for Kids!
This stunningly illustrated book guides teachers and children through preparing raw, vegan, and delicious snacks. With step-by-step instructions provided by magical fairies, even the most hardened vegetable-despising child can be swayed. The beauty of this book is how simple, yet effective the recipes are, meaning less preparation work for the teacher and higher success rates for

the children. I use this book at home with my own daughter and she is becoming quite the little pro!

Chickpea Runs Away
Chickpea the cow lives in an overcrowded barn on a large farm. She watches as her friends and family are taken away to an uncertain fate. One day, the farmer leads Chickpea and all the rest of the cows outdoors to a scary-looking truck, and Chickpea knows she shouldn't go. Making a split-second decision, she leaps the fence and escapes into the woods. For the first time ever, Chickpea discovers the world outside the farm and, thanks to some delicious vegan pie, makes new friends who welcome her with loving hearts. Chickpea's story is inspired by many real-life cases of runaway cows and teaches that animals have more awareness than most give them credit for.

T-Veg the Story of the Crunching Dinosaur
Reginald the T-Rex is a fun-loving character who is proud to claim to his dinosaur family and friends that he is an herbivore. Even when they mock and dismiss him for being different, he stays true to who he is and decides to run away instead of change. Shortly after leaving, the view from his new settlement reveals that there is disaster heading towards the dinosaur clan and he races back to the rescue, showing how fast and how strong he was; despite being an herbivore. They apologised, welcomed him with open arms, and held a vegetable party in his honour. This book is a great way to show the vegan child that they are unique and that they should stick to their convictions. This book is also perfect for teaching children to accept anyone despite their differences. I have used it, a lot!

The Lion Who Wanted to Love
Similar to T-Veg, little Leo the lion is a proud herbivore and is consequently banished from his pride. He goes in search of some

new friends and finds himself helping others in the jungle in return for tasty, fruity treats. This is until one day when he found himself in deep danger on a mission to help a drowning cheetah. Upon seeing how he helped his friend and then how his friends helped him, his pride realised what a special little lion he was after all and welcomed him back into the pride embracing his herbivorous and compassionate ways.

What Vegan Kids Eat!

What Vegan Kids Eat! is the first book that celebrates the wide variety of foods that vegan children enjoy. It debunks the notion that vegan children suffer from a lack of delicious food options. The truth is quite the opposite! This fun, light-hearted book, full of bold colours and friendly illustrations, is ideal for parents and teachers who wish to teach their children that being vegan is not only healthy and good for the animals but also delicious and fun.

Dave Loves Pigs

This wonderful book examines the characteristics of animals and questions why people eat them. Dave is a quirky monster from far, far away who happily discusses many fun and interesting facts about non-human animals. Dave simply loves all animals on Earth and believes that no one should harm them. This book is ideal for teaching the important message that animals are here with us and not for us.

Eating the Alphabet

A beautifully illustrated book that shows all of the fruits and vegetables that are available to us from A-Z. Although this book is not directly about veganism, it is one of many that promote healthy food and add interest to subject of healthy eating. This book, and others like it, will add value to the lessons surrounding health and vegan children can show off their favourites with pride, perhaps even seeing which food favourites they have in common with their peers.

Lena of Vegitopia and the Mystery of the Missing Animals: A Vegan Fairy Tale

Lena is forced onto a mission to save the animals who have been taken from her to be eaten. She harnesses the power of the veggies to rescue and set them free in this great action book. Lena is a brave leading character who stands up for her friends and also for what is right. There are many lessons to be learnt for all children in this exciting and action packed story.

That's Not My Momma's Milk!

This simple yet highly emotive and effective book shows the precious bond between animal mothers and their offspring. It teaches compassion and understanding with regards to babies drinking the milk made for them by their own mothers. It teaches that no one should break that sacred bond between a nursing newborn and its mother, as the dairy industry unfortunately does.

Vivi the Supervegan

This stunningly illustrated book carries such a sweet message and will be enjoyed by all those who read it, both young and old. The instinctive bond between children and animals is so beautifully portrayed within this unique story. Vivi is a brilliant character who can change people's hearts and minds with her superpowers, spreading vegan joy wherever she goes. A heart-warming read with purpose and powers, what more could you wish for?

These are just a few books that I have bought since becoming vegan. I know them inside and out and my family and I love them. Even I was just astonished when I typed "vegan kids books" into a search engine at the sheer volume of books that are now available. Please feel free to do your own research and purchase those that you feel would suit your class most. If you do not have at least a couple of vegan-related books in your class library, and larger whole school library, you are doing a disservice to your vegan child and wider class who may wish to learn more about their friends.

I recently read an article on LGBT literature, or lack thereof, in schools by Laura Tsabet, the assistant head of English at Redbridge Community School in Southampton and it struck a chord with me,

> "If we judiciously select LGBT fiction for our school libraries, we can provide our students with inspirational role models and the platform for understanding and accepting their own and other's sexuality. Yes, budgets are tight. But we owe it to our students."[75]

Your vegan child deserves to look in a library at their school and find vegan literature, not only to see themselves represented in wider society, but also to provide, as Laura has so eloquently put it, that crucial platform for understanding and acceptance.

Vegan Inclusive Policies to be Added to your School Policy Book

Below are a few examples of amendments that I believe you should make as soon as you discover that there are vegan children at your school. When writing policies, the wording is extremely important and must convey simply that you are either implementing immediately or are working towards a specific goal. You can of course make your own as each school has their own style of policy writing. The examples provided are guides that I hope you will find useful. The importance of adding this element of inclusion to your whole school policy shows that you are taking the matter seriously and that all Governors, Senior Leadership Team (SLT) members, and parents are on board with working towards and promoting a vegan-inclusive environment across the whole school.

Example 1:

At _____ we believe that each child who identifies as vegan deserves the right to be educated using methods which are inclusive. We aim to make our school as vegan-inclusive as possible and will endeavour to teach topics and use language deemed appropriate.

Example 2:

We at _____ understand the trauma triggers that a vegan child experiences and will work towards eliminating these from our daily practice. In doing so, we will avoid topics and language that the vegan child may find upsetting and will instead concentrate our efforts into teaching the key skills necessary through carefully thought out topics, stories, and experiences.

Example 3:

We here at _____ believe that each child deserves to feel safe and valued; this extends to vegan children also. We understand that vegan children see the world through very different eyes to the majority of the world, but we value their opinion and will work towards creating a fully vegan-inclusive school. Each year we will look at our topics, trips, activities, and stories ensuring that they are suitable for the entire class and will not trigger negative thoughts or disrupt the learning potential of the vegan child.

Example 4:

We at _____ will teach vegan-friendly topics throughout the full year that a vegan child spends in a class. The class teacher in that year will have training and a full understanding of what "vegan" means in order to be as inclusive as possible. We respect their belief system and will work in accordance with that.

CHAPTER 3:

What General Benefits Might You See?

~~~~~~

"We can't lie around on the couch eating French fries and
candy bars and expect our kids to eat carrots and run
around the block."
–Michelle Obama[76]

Healthy Relationship with Food

What I have found startling since working in and visiting primary schools, secondary schools, S.E.N. (Special Educational
Needs) schools, and even when taking my daughter to her local
gymnastics class, is the amount of rubbish that goes into the
average child's body. It's certainly not done in a malicious way; I
said there would be no judgement in this guidebook and I meant
it. I know that these educators love their children and do want
the best for them, but even schools with the "Healthy School"
stamp of approval award feed the children cereals at breakfast
club where at least 39g per 100g is sugar, as well as sweets, choc-

olates, biscuits, and of course animal products that are high in fat, saturated fat, and salts. It is done because everyone does it; it is the norm. More often than not, these educating houses will squeeze in a piece of fruit or some vegetable somewhere in the day, but children tend not to go for it, and looking at Michelle Obama's logic, why would they? I believe the whole system needs an overhaul. The educators need educating and we should be demanding more of our governments in the way of legislation.

As popular television chef and restaurateur Jamie Oliver says,

> "Imagine a world where children were fed tasty and nutritious, real food at school from the age of 4 to 18. A world where every child was educated about how amazing food is, where it comes from, how it affects the body and how it can save their lives."[77]

As mentioned in Chapter 1, health is one of the huge contributing factors to a family or child choosing to go vegan. Let's think about your role, and your day, as an educator and how different your day would be if, for example, the children in your class all came in after eating a fruit and vegetable packed smoothie, a sugar-free cereal served with fortified almond milk topped with seeds, and for snack they had fruit, nuts, and lemon water followed by a lunch of organic high fibre, high protein grains, vegetables, pluses, fruits, nuts, and legumes. Would they be bouncing off the walls? Would they be able to concentrate more? Would they have the energy to plough through the day? Would they be obese? Would you get more from them? Would you see a higher level of cognition?

What if you worked with children in a special needs school where children already had cognitive functions that make access to learning more difficult? What differences would you see with dietary changes? I have seen children and young adults with Autism and ADHD (Attention Deficit Hyperactivity Disorder) being fed cordial filled with sugar and artificial sweeteners change their calm behaviour twenty minutes after their drink almost like an alarm has gone off. They're in crisis, yet the professionals working alongside them were completely oblivious to the connection, more often than not asking, "Where did that come from?" as the child is being ushered into a safe space to calm down.

At gymnastics class, dance class, or any physical activity sports team that you may lead, imagine if you fed or even just encouraged the children to eat huge bowls of quinoa, wholemeal rice, edamame beans, blueberries, avocado, lentils, and vegetables topped with seeds; absolute bowls of goodness instead of sweets, bacon butties, or deep-fried chips. Imagine the greatness, imagine the performance. What a difference this would make. This should be the norm. World class athletes recognise this and we should be working harder to change our current norm, setting better examples, and changing the status quo as we go. As previously mentioned, one person can make a huge difference as you connect with other likeminded folk of the same thinking. Once again, we should not simply continue to do something because that is the way that it has always been done. Our children crave the wrong types of food and we provide it. Sweets, crisps, and chocolates are not seen by most of society as occasional treats anymore. This used to be the mindset of our grandparents after the Second World War, when rationing encouraged the population to be mindful and grateful for food. It's why they will still say, "It's just a little treat" even though it's not really applicable anymore. With the growth of 24-hour supermarkets, and such extensive choices, our children have learnt to demand and expect sweet treats daily, and even as a parent who can say "no" at home, we are powerless at school. Our children deserve better and I know as a teacher that you would absolutely agree with that sentiment.

There are of course exceptions, but, the vegan child in your classroom will likely have eaten bowls of good food, miso ramen, hummus, and rainbow salads for most, if not all of their life, and it is their norm. . Once you become vegan, a deeper respect for what fuels your body takes precedence over social norms. For example, my daughter has never stepped foot in any of the most notorious fast food establishments and sees them as "gross," to use her own word. Something else to think about is leaving their recognisable logos and catchphrases out of your classroom vocabulary altogether.

I fully appreciate that a child may come into your class who does not have a steady home life and may not have eaten breakfast but whilst they are in your care, you are their font of knowledge. They may not have had the best start in life and fast food may be all that they know, but you can encourage them to dream about a better and healthier future. Unfortunately, childhood malnutrition is not unique to the UK. It is something that the first lady of the United States Michelle Obama tried to eradicate as she wrote in her 2018 autobiography, Becoming:

> "Sam [Michelle's Live in Chef] also had an educated perspective on food and health issues, namely how the food industry marketed processed foods to families in the name of convenience and how that was having severe public health consequences"[78]

Michelle Obama launched the "Let's Move" project with the aim of encouraging the nation to take an interest in food, grow their own food, and cook with fresh ingredients. I am hoping that this project has a long-lasting effect despite the fact that the Obamas no longer live in the White House. It was refreshing to see such a prominent political figure advocating for this.

I recently calculated that with 52 weeks in the year, and 30 children in my daughter's class, if you take away the holidays, there is at least one birthday "sweet treat" coming home per week. And, oddly enough, when I mentioned the fact that I wished for my daughter to have less sugar at her before-and-after school club, I felt as though I was the one who was being awkward. To be more inclusive for the vegan child, you can encourage a healthier atmosphere in your classroom. Share healthy snacks, talk about healthy foods and their benefits, and not just when a healthy eating topic comes up. Certainly, try to avoid eating crisps or chocolates when the children can see you. I said there was to be no judgment and I am not expecting you to change your lifestyle outside of class, and yes sugar is sometimes vegan, if the bone char is left out, but at all times when you are in school you are a professional who has thirty pairs of eyes watching every move that you make. Please consider avoiding sweets as a congratulatory prize, they will value a certificate more and it lasts much longer. I couldn't believe that my daughter was offered sweets after receiving her first ever swimming certificate; the certificate and badge alone should have been enough. Perhaps opt for the vegan meal one day a week so you can discuss it with your vegan child and comment on how delicious it was for all of the class to hear. Maybe drink water, not coffee, and lots of it! Eating plant-based is such a powerful life changing and life affirming step to take and so, for the child to feel understood and supported by you, not only makes them feel special but you also have the opportunity to embrace it yourself, improving your own energy levels and lifestyle whilst also being that positive influence on the other children. This in turn benefits them and their health too. It's a win-win situation.

Recently, I was invited to take part in a BBC Five Live radio programme scheduled due to the fact that a young, teenage girl had been interviewed by the mainstream media saying that she was using veganism as a way to hide her eating disorder. I completely agree with author and psychologist Casey T. Taft when he wrote in his book *Millennial Vegan*:[79]

"There is no connection between wanting to minimize the harm we do to animals and having an eating disorder. In other words, going vegan for the animals does not place one at greater risk of developing an eating disorder. In fact, I believe that it's quite the opposite."

The main point made throughout this radio segment was that if you have an eating disorder, you are likely to use any excuse possible to hide your disorder whether its adherence to a vegan diet, the Atkins diet, or a paleo diet. This is especially important for your older children if, out of the blue, they decide to go vegan and concerns regarding an eating disorder have already been flagged up. If they seem to be refusing food because they are now "vegan," please ensure that you talk to them about their veganism and determine that they are doing it for the right reasons. It will become quite apparent whether or not they are doing it for the right outcomes, especially after reading this guidebook.

Impressionable young people who suffer from an eating disorder may turn to veganism due to the fact that it has been documented that there is a high percentage chance that a person will initially lose weight if they switch from a full, typical western diet to a whole foods plant-based diet. This is because they are cutting out a lot of fat, processed foods, takeaways, and improving their health. They may also take up physical exercise for the first time in a long time. Because losing weight is one of the positive side effects of the whole foods plant-based diet, many celebrities have endorsed it in magazines, although to be honest, they are nearly always just plant-based and not actually vegan. For those young and impressionable readers, they will see this and use it as an excuse to further their disorder. What must be kept in perspective though is that if you become vegan for the wrong reasons, more often than not, you may end up doing it incorrectly and that's where issues of malnourishment may come into play.

Upon going vegan, my relationship with food increased positively to new heights because I was all of a sudden reading packages, ingredients, health and medical journals, asking for blood tests, and learning about the different food groups and their nutritional values. I had an awesome head chef, Ismail, at my restaurant who was always talking about the best plant-based foods with the highest and most dense nutritional value. In fact, to this day I still alternate spirulina and chlorella daily in our family smoothies and smile to myself thinking about his encyclopaedic brain. That is how you do veganism properly because it is not a diet, it is an awakening. Once you are awake to its benefits, you find yourself constantly wanting to improve the health and life of those around you and your own too, completely contradicting the mindset of someone with an eating disorder. It is your duty as their carer to spot the difference and having read this guidebook you will now be able to separate the two.

Included Child/ren

The benefits of becoming a vegan-inclusive class for the vegan child will be immeasurable. They will be confident, forthcoming, and engaged. The older they get, the more important it will be for them to feel that way as differences seem to be so much more of an issue in teenage years. You will be more aware of your vegetarian children, your religious children, English as an Additional Language and Special Educational Needs and Disability children as you stop, reflect, and take another look at how inclusive your practice really is and whether your classroom setting fully reflects that.

Your children will be grateful, and you know there is no better feeling. You have taught them to be proud of who they are and what they are as well as how to write using connectives. I still enjoy receiving messages from children's parents who I had taught over a decade ago, filling me in on their journeys and successes. They would not bother unless I had made a real impact on their lives and genuinely believed that I care, and I do. Children will always remember that teacher who went the extra mile to include them. You finish the year with an enormous sense of wellbeing, as a positive role model to the children you've taught and who will remember your example for life.

Coinciding with the rising global vegan population, so too are uninvited cases of children being bullied at school simply because of the fact that they are vegan. The editor of Waitrose Food magazine was asked to leave his job in 2018 after it emerged he'd suggested a television series on "Killing vegans, one by one"[80] in response to a freelance journalist who had pitched features on plant-based recipes. My mother recently attended a luncheon where the local caterer had responded to the host's question, "What can you do for vegans?" with the answer, "Shoot them in the head." These comments came from adults and businessmen who should know better. When it comes to children, who we know have the capacity to be cruel without fully understanding the consequences, it is no wonder that vegan children are becoming targets for bullying.

I am appalled by recent cases reported in the UK, about two children, Dante, 14 and Louie, 12. The reason why I feel it is important to discuss these two children is to highlight the realities that exist within our schooling systems and to encourage prevention strategies to stop them from happening again, potentially under your watch.

Dante was attacked in October 2018 and suffered with symptoms consistent with post-concussion syndrome. He was attacked purely because he was vegan by two other students in his Welsh home town. Dante was head butted, pinned down, had his wrists restrained, and was constantly punched so that his attackers could force meat down his throat.

In January 2017, Louie, a twelve-year-old boy was found hanged at his home in Hertfordshire after enduring years of bullying due to his veganism. Before his death, Louie had to tolerate having meat thrown at him and began to eat alone outside instead of in his canteen.

There are many lessons to be learnt from these two heart wrenching stories. As with most safeguarding and protection policies, it unfortunately takes something horrific to happen before legislation in enforced. An example of this is with the introduction of the 2003 UK *Every Child Matters* document introduced in response to the murder of Victoria Climbié. As far as I am concerned, the two stories above are horrific enough to warrant legislative change which sees vegan education included into the national curriculum, but no such thing has been implemented to date. Although veganism is vaguely covered under the Equality Act of 2010, which is what I used as my basis for demanding vegan food became available for my daughter at her school, it still is not specific enough. The word "vegan" does not appear in this act. This vagueness and inconsistency has to be addressed and soon to avoid tragedies like these happening again.

It is left only up to vegan advocates like me who are putting our cases forward for vegan-inclusion, but there's only so much we can do. It is inevitably left up to you to teach about, mention, and normalise veganism to the best of your ability. In doing so, you will be bridging gaps, strengthening understanding, and encouraging meaningful relationships.

Good Influence on Other Children

I have unfortunately seen many vegan children crying on You-Tube videos when they despair with the world around them. I have seen my daughter heartbroken watching her only female cousin, who she adores, stomp on ants and I have seen many young, vegan activists come together at peaceful protests determined to save the world. The one thing that all of these children have in common is that they are all incredibly empathetic. I often see them wearing the tee shirt with the slogan "In a world where you can be anything, be kind." These children have nailed it. That is not to say that non-vegan children are not kind, but there is a lot to be said for the core values which vegan children hold and how they act in wider society because of them. You only have to look as far as teenager Greta Thunberg, the Swedish, vegan, climate activist, to be blown away by her qualities and her positive influence.

At the primary school where I gained my Qualified Teacher Status, and years later where I was promoted to Senco, my remarkable head teacher Ms. Ashton once told a story about *The 20th Child*. This was a theoretical story regarding the innate behaviour of children that she had learnt at a head teacher training event.

The 20th Child

Next to a line of school children waiting to enter a room, there was a piece of rubbish on the floor. The first few children would nonchalantly walk straight past it, it wouldn't even occur to them to pick it up. The next few children might acknowledge it and then kick it out of their way. The next few children might pick it up and put it in the bin, but only did this as a sense of duty because their teacher was watching. The final few children may pick it up and put it in the bin but only in the hope that someone saw and would praise them for it. Then there is the 20th Child, the child who puts it into the bin without any fuss or anyone watching, and they do so because they believe, innately, that it is the right thing to do.

Since becoming vegan, I can say hand on heart, that I am a better person than I was. I cannot speak for all vegans on this matter, but for me personally this is true. I am less selfish, I volunteer more, I'm more environmentally aware, and I don't shout about good deeds that I have done, I just get on with it. I don't even pick or buy flowers anymore because I see and feel their importance for the insects and wouldn't want to get in the way of that. The 20th Child may very well have been born with the empathic gene, but what children see and do will ultimately inform what kind of person they are going to be. My daughter witnesses all that I do and the morals that I hold, the exercise I undertake, the food I eat, the sustainable and eco changes that I have made, the food bank deliveries that I have donated, and she will be watching her teachers just as closely. As Casey Taft wrote in Millennial Vegan, I strive to be "morally consistent."[79] It is because of this consistency that my daughter knows how compassionate, thoughtful, and kind people behave and why she alone when out shopping with her teachers was perfectly able and confident enough to ask if they could buy the yellow peppers that were loose as opposed to the ones wrapped in plastic. Thankfully they agreed, telling me afterwards that she had said, "It's how mummy does it."

If you teach children to respect everyone and everything, regardless of their race, gender, or species from a very early age, you are setting them up to avoid conflict and live harmoniously. This enabled my daughter to be able to explain in a gentle way to her cousin a few months back that "ants don't like to be stomped on" and that they will have been "frightened" of her. I heard my niece use that exact same sentence recently when regaling us with a tale about a spider and it warmed my heart. Positive influence is something that should be at the forefront of all of our actions at school and in the greater wide world.

"At the root of speciesism, racism, sexism, ableism, ageism, homo- and trans-antagonism, and other isms is the notion that some individuals are lesser than others. If we can get people to recognise that none of us are any higher, better, or more deserving than any other, we can bring about great change."

–Casey Taft[81]

More Compassionate Classroom – Humane Education

"The world becomes what we teach."
–Institute for Humane Education[82]

Many of the points that I have made in this guidebook can be considered part of the Humane Education curriculum. Humane Education as a concept was first moulded into a campaign in the United States at the beginning of the 1900's. In 1905, William O. Stillman of the American Humane Association and professional educator Stella H. Preston formed the New York Humane Education Committee and since then it has been growing in momentum.

Humane education is different to animal welfare education as it also encompasses the belief that we should be taught from a very early age how to respect ourselves, one another, the animals and the environment equally. Humane educators believe these skills are fundamental to a sustainable and peaceful world and should be held in the same regard as core subjects such as numeracy, literacy, and science. Humane education is invaluable as it also provides children with the skills necessary to problem solve as well as crucial lessons in how to deal with modern sustainability issues.

Lessons in respect, compassion, critical thinking, and sustainability would form the backbone of each global curriculum. Educating and empowering the youth with social responsibility will inevitably lead to a more conscientious, compassionate, and caring society. By uniting to eliminate our most desperate situations such as war, global warming, prejudice, deforestation, and animal agriculture, imagine what humanity could accomplish.

Humane education encompasses a vegan-inclusive education and is becoming better known amongst educators as an exciting direction to take. Some head teachers may be reluctant to travel down this path for a fear that it would bring attainment down, but there is a growing network of teachers who consider themselves humane educators. They have been inspired by the Finnish model of education which has shown perfectly well that you can achieve high attainment whilst also churning out a population who consider themselves happy. The Finnish National Agency for Education, which sets core curricula requirements, stated their goal for basic education is, "to support pupils' growth toward humanity and ethically responsible membership of society and to provide them with the knowledge and skills needed in life."[83]

Teachheart.org is a fantastic resource for any teacher who wishes to incorporate a humane education which includes over forty free lesson plans to use, all based on a humane curriculum. And the topics outlined in the previous chapter are all examples of how a humane education could look, because let's face it, with the direction that the world is heading in now everyone, but especially teachers, have got to seriously up their compassionate game.

Animalvoice.org is equally wonderful and contains a wealth of humane education resources that have been rolled out in South Africa. Their excellent Caring Classrooms teaching platform is completely free and contains the first-ever teacher's guide to a humane education.

CHAPTER 4:

Examples of Lesson Plans Introducing the Class to Veganism

In the early years setting (4-5 years), children have around a five-minute concentration span before they start to switch off. A good story helps extend this, especially if it is read well. This simple lesson gets straight to the point with a character that they can remember fondly.

(4-5 Years)	
Learning Objective	We are learning what it means to be vegan.
Introduction	Today's special lesson is about vegan people. You may have someone in your class who is vegan. Vegans are people, just like us, but they love animals so much that... • They don't use animals. • They don't eat animals or their products. • They don't visit them when they are in cages.
Main Lesson and Activity	Let's take a closer look at our friend Reginald the T-Rex who is also a vegan. Whilst listening to the story, ask the children to think really hard about what the message of the story is. Teacher reads the book T-Veg the Story of the Crunching Dinosaur and accentuates the point that, although he eats differently, everyone loves him the same. Then ask the children what the message in that story was?

Plenary	Try some delicious foods that are vegan-friendly.
	Meanwhile, the vegan child might be able to answer some questions about being vegan from their peers.

As a follow up the next day you could read the book The Lion Who Wanted Love and talk about the similarities between the main characters. If the children say "They are both vegan," you know that your lesson from the previous day was a success.

Key Stage 1 (5-7 years) children are able to understand a little more regarding where their food comes from and how it is produced. They will also have more life experience than the younger children and will have probably visited some of the animal industry establishments mentioned previously. This lesson clearly sets out what it means to be vegan in a clear and illustrated form.

(5-7 Years)	
Learning Objective	We are learning what it means to be vegan.
Introduction	Today's special lesson is about vegan people. You may have someone in your class who is vegan. Vegans are people, just like us, but they love animals so much that... • They don't use animals. • They don't eat animals or their products. • They don't visit them when they are in cages.
Main Lesson and Activity	Children are provided with photographs of activities that use animals such as a zoo, a bear circus performer, and an aquarium. Add some pictures of other fun activities such as roller skating, swimming, using a trampoline, etc.

	and ask the children to split these into two categories of vegan and non-vegan activities. This activity will show that even though vegans choose not to go to some places, they can still have awesome fun doing other stuff that doesn't involve animals.
	Do the same with food pictures. Ensure that the pictures chosen will not upset the vegan child in the class – e.g. chicken goujon as opposed to a chicken carcass.
	Again, the children will see that fun options are still available to the vegan child even though they choose alternatives.
	At this point, it's also fun to see if children can say the words quinoa, seitan, and couscous. The lesson should be light, with a focus on the children "choose" not to eat that as opposed to "they aren't allowed."
Plenary	Try some delicious foods that are vegan-friendly.
	Meanwhile, the vegan child might be able to answer some questions about being vegan from their peers.

As a follow up later that day, read a book such as *The Lion Who Wanted Love* or *T-Veg the Story of the Crunching Dinosaur* and further accentuate the point that although he eats differently, everyone loves him the same.

Older children (8-11 years) are certainly able to have a reasoned discussion on this issue. By the end of this lesson, they will understand what being vegan means and will have a deeper understanding of why a person chooses to identify as such.

(4-11 Years)	
Learning Objective	We are learning that humans are herbivores.
Introduction	Stick up two large pictures, one herbivorous dinosaur and one carnivorous dinosaur, next to one another. Ask the children to point out their similarities and differences and write them underneath each picture. This will differ with each age group. It could look like this. **Carnivore:** super sharp teeth, really super fast, scary, sharp claws **Herbivore:** blunt teeth, fast-ish, more slow, gentle, no claws

Main Lesson and Activity	Ask which one do you think humans are closest to?
	The children will be encouraged to have a chat and a think with each other to further stimulate their brains.
	Obviously, humans relate more to the herbivorous side, so this is when you say it is okay for a human to be herbivorous!
	Introduce the word **vegan** at this point. Instead of calling humans herbivores, you can call them vegan because they only eat plants but they are still big, strong, and healthy like the herbivorous dinosaur.
	You could also show land mammals, such as rhinos or elephants, at this point. If you have time, show the strength that comes from plants alone. You may also compare the teeth or claws of herbivores and carnivores by cutting out a selection and asking the children to group them.
	Then read the book *T-Rex the Vegetarian Dinosaur* which is linked in with the conversation you've just had. (Feel free to swap out the word vegetarian with vegan where it appears once but other than that the story is a **perfect** way to end the lesson. It is a great resource.

Plenary	Discuss that even though we are herbivorous, some humans choose to eat meat and they are called omnivores. Just because we can, does it mean that we should?
	This is an extension of thinking and by using clever questioning; especially with older children you can get some insightful conversations.

Although these four lesson plans were written with specific age groups in mind, there is nothing to say that you can't swap and switch elements from each. Edit and use how you wish. You know your class better than anyone and which activities will be best suited. You could even simply ask the children to "draw a vegan" as a starter activity and see what their misconceptions are. A lesson like this about misconceptions are always fun and carry with them important messages about generalising. These lessons are guidelines and ideas which do not need to be followed to the letter. Please feel free to make temporary wall displays out of your outcomes and remember the important thing is that you are incorporating veganism into the curriculum in your now vegan-inclusive classroom.

CONCLUSIONS

I'd like to thank you sincerely for taking the time to read this guidebook. My hope is that you feel more confident now as you go forth and create your vegan-inclusive classroom. This may take a while as there is a lot to consider, but please be patient and, if you keep at it, I guarantee it will become second nature to you soon enough.

Eventually most countries' legal and political systems will catch up so that vegan-inclusion is an expected part of all public and private sector legislation. Thankfully you will have had a massive head start after having read this guidebook, which means that many children will already start to benefit from the hard work that you put in, you may even become a specialist in this area! As a vegan, mother, and teacher I have to tell you the fact that you have purchased this book or have at least taken the time to read it, is very much appreciated. The gratitude from the children and parents whose lives you are about to improve, and show respect for, will be long-lasting. I cannot express enough how wonderful it feels to have a teacher or teaching assistant, well anyone at the school, pay an interest in or ask me a question about veganism. I try to be as approachable as I can, but not all parents might be that way. I would recommend opening that line of dialogue and show willingness to engage. My daughter's lovely teaching assistant approached asked me about eggs the other day and it was a magical moment for me.

Please do remember though, that each vegan child is different and may have different views to those that I have outlined; I have tried not to generalise. However, we are all still individuals and, as you plan for the vegan children in your classroom, you should get to know them and discuss their views with them so that you can not only become vegan-inclusive, but also use what you have learnt about them and their interests to enhance their learning.

Teaching can be difficult and pretty full on with so many legislative changes and demands being made all of the time. This is one area though, where you do have enough time to get your head around it before the majority of your class is vegan. With each child who enters your classroom, you'll find yourself more aware and more open to implementing the suggestions as described in this guidebook. This social justice movement is growing day by day and, if you can understand the reasons why and know how to embrace it from reading this guidebook, then my work here is done. We are living in a pivotal time where vegans such as Corey Booker hold high office in the USA. In addition, Emma Hurst for the Animal Justice Party (AJP) recently took a second NSW seat for her party, joining fellow AJP politician Mark Pearson in Australia. New Zealand Prime Minister Jacinda Ardern wants to prioritise national well-being over GDP and Zuzana Caputova, a liberal environmental activist, has been elected as the first female president of Slovakia. Vegan members of parliament Kerry McCarthy MP and Christina Rees MP are regularly hosting vegan and vegetarian all-party parliamentary group meetings in Westminster to which I have attended and met some real game changers in the process. As well as this, I am due to speak at the Oxford University Animal Ethics School in the summer regarding vegan-inclusion in schools and Ed Winters, also known as Earthling Ed, who is a passionate public speaker and founder of SURGE activism in the UK, was just recently invited to Harvard to share his thoughts. Wonderful and supportive websites such as "Grow Up Vegan" and vegan festivals such as the UK Vegan Campout, which hosted over seven thousand people at their last event, are growing in numbers to assist those making the lifestyle change. Veganism, as a movement, is more prevalent than ever before. Your choice is either to embrace it whilst you are at work or deny it, but you and I both know that the latter is always going to be the choice that a fully inclusive teacher will take.

To further understand how far changes in your own behaviour and classroom ethos will go towards the successful implementation of a humane education and just how integral your role as teacher is in shaping our society, I refer to a research paper undertaken by Unti and DeRosa, who wrote:[84]

"Providing teachers with the necessary training, tools, and motivation will require a re-examination of traditional humane education methodology. Standard practices such as classroom visits and shelter tours typically relegate the classroom teacher to the role of bystander, involved marginally at most in the presentation of humane concepts and lessons. Such approaches can reinforce the notion of humane education as a novelty or special interest, exclusively the purview of the animal protection organisation, and both separate from and subordinate to core curricula. Making schools partners in the propagation of a humane ethic will involve, at

the very least, cultivating ongoing working relationships with teachers and administrators."

When asked over the years, as I am sure that you have
been, "Why did you became a teacher?" Your answer may have
included a love for children, a desire to make a difference, to
contribute to society or something similar. Having now read and
learnt all that you have about a vegan-inclusive education, perhaps you will begin to see the curriculum as your opportunity
to do all of those things, and much more. You can use it as a
powerful tool for educating about positive social change. Yes, the
curriculum is packed with practical and essential quantitative
and concrete information handy for a future in economics or
industry. But, you and I both know that real success in life comes
with making relationships, happy mental health, seeing the joy
in a rainbow or helping someone in need. It is the qualitative,
reflective, respectful, hopeful, honest, and peaceful areas of human society that our children require the most lessons in order
to navigate successfully through adulthood, and that too has to
be taught, by you. Perhaps you are at a point in your career where
you needed to be reminded of this, possibly now you will worry a
little less about data and more on the natural world. Perhaps your
answer as to why you became a teacher will now change forever.

RESOURCES

Websites

YouTube, Dairy is Scary
https://www.youtube.com/watch?v=UcN7SGGoCNI

YouTube, Bite Size Vegan, Vegan Kids Videos
https://www.youtube.com/watch?v=GDEc87fo-mio&list=PLmIqdlomtuStMwQ9KWEE8Nn5GyK6vNqz2

One Green Planet, Why "Eating Just Fish" Still Harms the Environment
https://www.onegreenplanet.org/environment/eating-just-fish-harms-the-environment

Ruby Roth interview
https://www.facebook.com/livekindlyco/videos/Vegan-author-responds-to-mainstream-media/607119172969994

The Ostrich Effect: The Truth We Hide from Ourselves | Ed Winters | TEDxLundUniversity
https://www.youtube.com/watch?v=nrVEYTSe-o8

Crisis in the Slaughterhouse
https://www.theguardian.com/commentisfree/2018/nov/19/christmas-crisis-kill-dinner-work-abattoir-industry-psychological-physical-damage

Crisis in the Slaughterhouse
https://www.veganlabs.com/theveginning/issue-4/the-threats-to-public-health-and-safety-for-people-living-near-factory-farms

Slaughterhouse Pollution

https://www.onegreenplanet.org/environment/how-slaughter-houses-are-polluting-the-planet

Is Honey Vegan?

https://veganuary.com/myths/bees/?gclid=EAIaIQobCh-MI7MDRn6eY4AIVqrvtCh3S6AX3EAAYASAAEgIz7PD_BwE

The Vegan Society, The Egg Industry

https://www.vegansociety.com/go-vegan/egg-industry

Viva! Nutrition posters

https://vivashop.org.uk/collections/materials/category_wall-charts-posters-stickers

Grow up Vegan, Support for Vegan Children and Parents

https://www.growupvegan.com/

Newspaper articles from our vegan school food victory!

https://www.manchestereveningnews.co.uk/news/greater-man-chester-news/vegan-free-school-meals-bury-15254775

https://metro.co.uk/2018/10/09/mum-used-human-rights-act-to-get-school-to-serve-vegan-food-8019928/

Films

Earthlings (2005)
What the Health (2017)
Forks Over Knives (2011)
Okja (2017)
Dominion (2018)
Land of Hope and Glory (2017)

Fat, Sick & Nearly Dead (2010)
Cowspiracy: The Sustainability Secret (2014)
Simply Raw: Reversing Diabetes in 30 Days (2009)
Speciesism: The Movie (2013)
Peaceable Kingdom (2004)
Live and Let Live (2013)
Game Changers (2019)

Legislative Documents

HM Treasury, Published 8 September 2003
https://www.gov.uk/government/publications/every-child-matters

Equality Act 2010: Guidance. (2013). GOV.UK.
https://www.gov.uk/guidance/equality-act-2010-guidance.

GOV.CO.UK, Eligibility for the school milk subsidy scheme
- milk consumed from 1 August 2017 [online] 26 June 2017,
27/06/2018,
https://www.gov.uk/guidance/eligibility-for-the-school-milk-subsidy-scheme-milk-consumed-from-1-august-2017

DEPARTMENT OF HEALTH, Next Steps for Nursery Milk
Government Response [online] © Crown copyright 2014 Published to gov.uk, 27/06/2018
https://assets.publishing.service.gov.uk/government/uploads/system/uploads/attachment_data/file/298196/Nursery_Milk_Response..pdf

School Milk.
https://www.gov.uk/guidance/eligibility-for-the-school-milk-subsidy-scheme-milk-consumed-from-1-august-2017

https://assets.publishing.service.gov.uk/government/uploads/system/uploads/attachment_data/file/298196/Nursery_Milk_Response..pdf

Vegan-Inclusive Plans

The Pond

Oscar and the Frog
Waring, G. (2010). *Oscar And the Frog*. Boston, MA: Houghton Mifflin.

Princess and the Frog
Clements, R., & Musker, J. (2009). *Princess and The Frog*. Walt Disney Animation Studios.

Oi Frog
Gray, K., & Field, J. (2014). *Oi Frog!* Hachette Children's Group.

The Wind and the Willows
Grahame, K., & Moore, I. (1908). *The Wind in the Willows*. Methuen.

The Frog Chorus
McCartney, P. (2019). *Paul McCartney and The Frog Chorus – We All Stand Together*. https://www.youtube.com/watch?v=A0fuVoSa3dc.

Jump, Frog, Jump
Kalan, R., & Barton, B. (1981). *Jump, Frog, Jump*. Pine Plains, NY: Live Oak Media.

In the Small Pond
Fleming, D., McFadden, J. & Dern, L. (2001). *In the Small, Small Pond.* Weston, CT: Weston Woods.

An Extraordinary Egg
Lionni, L. (1994). *An Extraordinary Egg (Big Book).* New York, NY: Scholastic.

Pond Walk
Wallace, N. (2011). *Pond Walk.* Two Lions.

Life in a Pond
Hammersmith, C. (2012). *Life in a Pond.* Mankato, MN: Capstone Press.

The Forest

Gruffalo
Donaldson, J., & Scheffler, A. (2019). *Gruffalo 20th Anniversary Edition.* Macmillan Children's Books; Main Market edition.

The Chronicles of Narnia
Lewis, C., & Baynes, P. (1956). *The Chronicles Of Narnia.* Geoffrey Bles (books 1–5), The Bodley Head (books 6–7), HarperCollins (current; worldwide).

Forest has a Song
VanDerwater, A. (2013). *Forest Has A Song: Poems.* Clarion Books.

A Bug's Life
Lasseter, J. (2019). *A Bug's Life.* United States: Walt Disney Pictures, Pixar Animation Studios.

Bambi
Hand, D. (1942). *Bambi*. United States: Walt Disney Productions.

Man Who Planted Trees
Man Who Planted Trees Assembly – Woodland Trust. (2019). *Woodlandtrust. Org. Uk*. https://www.woodlandtrust.org.uk/ get-involved/schools/mwpt-assembly/.

The Happiness Tree
English, D. (2018). *The Happiness Tree*. UK: Hygge Media.

A Tree Grows
A Listen Along Story Teaching Children The Value Of Patience. (2013). Image. https://www.youtube.com/watch?v=2zfpxajngtI.

The Sanctuary

Freedom Dance
Government, Z. (2014). Freedom Dance. https://www.youtube. com/watch?v=HL28tlVFy-A.

Long Walk to Freedom
Mandela, N. (2014). *Long Walk To Freedom*. Paw Prints.

Alive
Read, P. (2016). *Alive*. New York: Open Road Media.

Journey to Jo'burg
Naidoo, B. (2019). *Journey To Jo'burg*. [S.l.]: HarperCollins.

The Specials – Nelson Mandela (1984)
https://www.youtube.com/watch?v=AgcTvoWjZJU

The Bug Hotel

Friends of the Earth
The Bee Cause. (2018). *Cdn.Friendsoftheearth.Uk.* https://cdn.
friendsoftheearth.uk/sites/default/files/downloads/The%20
Bee%20Cause%20-%20a%20pack%20for%20educators.pdf.

Ugly Bug Ball
Ugly Bug Ball. (1963). Disney. https://www.youtube.com/watch?

Life of Insects
Attenborough, D. (2010). Life Of Insects: Life In The
Undergrowth. *BBC Earth.* https://www.youtube.com/
watch?v=uppwVyUd5S0.

We're Going on a Bear Hunt
Rosen, M. (1989). *We're Going on a Bear Hunt.* Helen Oxenbury.

James and the Giant Peach
Dahl, R. (1961). *James And The Giant Peach.* Alfred Knopf.

Superworm
Donaldson, J. (2013). *Superworm.* [S.l.]: Alison Green Books.

A Bug's Life
Lasseter, J. (1998). *A Bug's Life.* Pixar Animation Studios for
Walt Disney Pictures.

Monkey Puzzle
Donaldson, J. (2000). *Monkey Puzzle.* Macmillan Children's
Books; New Ed edition

The Swamp/The Bog

The Bog Baby
Willis, J., & Millward, G. (2008). *The Bog Baby.* Puffin.

We're Going on a Bear Hunt
Rosen, M. (1989). *We're Going On A Bear Hunt.* Helen Oxenbury.

Christmas in the Swamp
Christmas In The Swamp – KS2. (2018). *Stage Invaders.* https://www.stageinvaders.org/musicals/christmas-in-the-swamp.

Shrek
Adamson, A., & Jenson, V. (2001). *Shrek.* United States: DreamWorks Animation.

Bedtime at the Swamp
Crow, K. (2008). *Bedtime at the Swamp.* Harper Collins.

Life in the Swamp
Earth Touch. (2016). *Wildlife 360: Life in the Swamp.* https://www.youtube.com/watch?v=1rKU9XINM6c.

The Werewolf of Fever Swamp
Stine, R. (2015). *The Werewolf of Fever Swamp (Goosebumps).* 2nd ed. Scholastic.

Swamp Monster
Preller, J. (2015). *Swamp Monster (Scary Tales).* Feiwel & Friends.

Children's Books

Roth, R. (2013). *V is for Vegan.* Berkeley, CA: North Atlantic Books.

Bedford, E. (2016). *How to Eat a Rainbow: Magical Raw Vegan Recipes for Kids!* Danvers, MA: Vegan Publishers.

Colling, S. (2019). *Chickpea Runs Away.* Danvers, MA: Vegan Publishers.

Prasadam-Halls, S. (2017). *T-Veg the Story of the Crunching Dinosaur.* New York, NY: Harry N. Abrams.

Andreae, G. (1999). *The Lion Who Wanted Love.* Chicago, IL: Orchard Books.

Pollock, A. (2019). *What Vegan Kids Eat!* Danvers, MA: Vegan Publishers.

Patino, C. (2016). *Dave Loves Pigs.* Danvers, MA: Vegan Publishers.

Ehlert, L. (1996). *Eating the Alphabet.* Boston, MA: HMH Books for Young Readers.

Severin, S. (2014). *Lena of Vegitopia and the Mystery of the Missing Animals: A Vegan Fairy Tale.* Danvers, MA: Vegan Publishers.

Barcalow, J. (2017). *That's Not My Momma's Milk!* Danvers, MA: Vegan Publishers.

Newman, T. (2019). *Vivi the Supervegan.*

REFERENCES

1. Pantić, N., & Florian, L. (2015). Developing Teachers as Agents of Inclusion and Social Justice. *Education Inquiry*, 6 (3): 27311.
2. Hancox, D. (2018). The Unstoppable Rise of Veganism: How A Fringe Movement Went Mainstream. *Guardian*.
3. Plantbasednews.Org. (2019). *Veganism Skyrockets To 7% Of UK Population*, Says New Survey.
4. Sebba, J. 1997. What Works in Inclusive Education? *Barnardos*.
5. The Vegan Society. (2019). *Definition of Veganism*.
6. Regan, T. (2003). *Empty Cages*. Lanham, Maryland: Rowman & Littlefield.
7. Cooke, C. (2019). Factory farming is sweeping the U.K. *Civil Eats*.
8. Definition of Vegetarian. (2019). *Lexico Dictionaries*.
9. Definition of Speciesism. (2019). *Encyclopedia Britannica*.
10. Singer, P. (1975). *Animal Liberation: A New Ethics for Our Treatment of Animals*. Harper Collins.
11. Roth, R. (2012). *Vegan is Love*. Berkeley, California: North Atlantic Books.
12. Butler, J. (2009). The Fish Report: Why public health policy should promote plant omega-3 in preference to fish oils. *Vegetarian & Vegan Foundation*.
13. Sustainable Seafood | Industries. (2019). *World Wildlife Fund*.
14. Pittman, A. (2019). Why "eating just fish" still harms the environment. *One Green Planet*.
15. Keledjian, A., Brogan, G., Lowell, B., Warrenchuk, J., Enticknap, B., Shester, G., Hirshfield, M., & Cano-Stocco, D. (2014). Wasted catch: Unsolved problems in U.S. fisheries. *Oceana*.
16. High Quest Group. (2016). *Saving bees saving ourselves*.
17. Golden Blossom Honey. (2019). Learn bee facts, honey trivia, honey nutrition facts and more! *Goldenblossomhoney.Com*.
18. Katcher, J. (2019). *Fashion Animals*. Danvers, Massachusetts: Vegan Publishers.
19. Mann, C. (2018). *Vystopia: The Anguish of Being Vegan in A Non-Vegan World*. Communicate31 PTY Ltd.
20. Foer, J. (2009). *Eating Animals*. Hamish Hamilton.
21. Warley, J. (2018). Why we should ban animals from the circus. *Onekindplanet*.
22. Blais, S. (2014.) Space, how much is enough?" *Global Sanctuary for Elephants*.
23. PETA (2018). *Aquariums and marine parks*. https://www.peta.org/issues/animals-in-entertainment/zoos-pseudo-sanctuaries/aquariums-marine-parks/.
24. Rspca.Org.Uk. (2019). *Sentient beings*. https://www.rspca.org.uk/getinvolved/campaign/sentientbeings.
25. Mitchell, D. (2018). My beef with vegans says more about me than them. *Guardian*.
26. Roll, R. (2017). Podcast. *Cardiologist Kim Williams*, M.D. wants to eradicate heart disease. https://www.richroll.com/podcast/kim-williams/.
27. Larsson, S., Bergkvist, L., & Wolk, A. (2004). Milk and lactose intakes and ovarian cancer risk in the Swedish mammography cohort. *The American Journal of Clinical Nutrition*, 80 (5): 1353-1357.
28. Larsson, S., Virtamo, J., & Wolk, A. (2012). Dairy consumption and risk of stroke in Swedish women and men. *Stroke*, 43 (7): 1775-1780.

29. Yusoff, N., Mohd, A., Hampton, S., Dickerson, J., & Morgan, J. (2004). The effects of exclusion of dietary egg and milk in the management of asthmatic children: A pilot study. *Journal of The Royal Society for The Promotion of Health* 124 (2): 74-80.

30. Ghanim, H., Abuaysheh, S., Sia, C., Korzeniewski, K., Chaudhuri, A., Fernandez-Real, J., & Dandona, P. (2009). Increase in plasma endotoxin concentrations and the expression of toll-like receptors and suppressor of cytokine signaling-3 in mononuclear cells after a high-fat, high-carbohydrate meal: Implications for insulin resistance. *Diabetes Care*, 32 (12): 2281-2287.

31. Snyder, W. (2014). *The good, the bad and the ugly of inflammation.* Vanderbilt Medical Center. https://www.mc.vanderbilt.edu/vanderbiltmedicine/the-good-the-bad-and-the-ugly-of-inflammation/.

32. Esselstyn, C., Gendy, G., Doyle, J., Golubic, M., & Roizen, M. (2014). A way to reverse CAD?" *US National Library of Medicine National Institutes of Health*, 63(7):356-364b.

33. Who.Int. (2019). *Cardiovascular diseases.* https://www.who.int/health-topics/cardiovascular-diseases/.

34. Vegan Streams. (2011). *Dr. Neal Barnard: Plant-based diet IS our medicine.* https://www.youtube.com/watch?v=DrinoIFsztU.

35. Mills M. (2016). *Are humans designed to eat meat?* https://www.youtube.com/watch?v=sXj76A9hI-o.

36. Harari, Y. (2015). *Sapiens: A brief history of humankind.* New York, NY: Harper.

37. Roberts, W. (1990). We think we are one, we act as if we are one, but we are not one. *The American Journal of Cardiology*, 66 (10): 896.

38. House of Commons Library. (2018). *Obesity statistics.*

39. Macknin, M., Kong, T., Weier, A., Worley, S., Tang, A., Alkhouri, N., & Golubic, M. (2015). Plant-based, no-added-fat or American Heart Association diets: Impact on cardiovascular risk in obese children with hypercholesterolemia and their parents." *The Journal of Pediatrics*, 166 (4): 953-959.

40. Harari, Y. (2015). *Sapiens : A brief history of humankind.* New York: Harper.

41. Steinfeld, H., Gerber, P., Wassenaar, T., Castel, V., Rosales, M., de Haan, C. (2006). *Livestock's long shadow: Environmental issues and options.*

42. Hertwich, E., van der Voet, E., Suh, S., Tukker, A., Huijbregts M., Kazmierczyk, P., Lenzen, M., McNeely, J., & Moriguchi, Y. (2010). *Assessing the environmental impacts of consumption and production: Priority products and materials.* A report of the working group on the environmental impacts of products and materials to the International Panel for Sustainable Resource Management.

43. United Nations Environment Programme. (2017). *The emissions gap report.* Nairobi.

44. United States Environmental Protection Agency. (2017). *Understanding world warming potentials.*

45. FAO. (2011). World livestock 2011 – Livestock in food security. Rome.

46. PETA. (2019). *How much water does it take to make one steak?* https://www.peta.org/videos/meat-wastes-water/.

47. Mekonnen, M., & Hoekstra, A. (2010). *The green, blue and grey water footprint of farm animals and animal products. Value of water research report series no. 48.* UNESCO-IHE, Delft, the Netherlands.

48. Wasley, A., Davies, A. Adams, C., & Robbins, J. (2017). Dirty business: The livestock farms polluting the UK. *The Bureau of Investigative Journalism.*

49. Wasley, A., Harvey, F., & Davies, M. (2017). Serious farm pollution breaches rise in UK – and many go unprosecuted. *Guardian News and Media Limited.*

50. FAO. (2018). *The state of world fisheries and aquaculture: Meeting the sustainable development goals.* Rome. Licence: CC BY-NC-SA 3.0 IGO.
51. World Wildlife Fund. (2019). *Bycatch: A sad topic.* https://www.fishforward.eu/en/project/by-catch/.
52. Veganuary. (2019). *Myths: Isn't soya destroying the environment and rainforests though?* https://veganuary.com/myths/isnt-soya-destroying-the-environment-and-rainforests-though.
53. Cho, R. (2014). *Making progress on deforestation.* https://blogs.ei.columbia.edu/2014/06/23/making-progress-on-deforestation/.
54. Cappiello, J. (2017). *This one simple change will help countless wild animals.* https://mercyforanimals.org/this-one-simple-change-will-help-countless.
55. The Labour Party. (2018). *The green transformation: Labour's environment policy.* https://www.labour.org.uk/wp-content/uploads/2018/09/The-Green-Transformation-.pdf.
56. Vegan Calculator – The Vegan Web Designer. (2019). *Vegan Calculator.* http://thevegancalculator.com/#calculator.
57. Loria, J. (2016). Moooove over milk... millennials are done with dairy. *Mercy for Animals.* https://mercyforanimals.org/moooove-over-milk-millennials-are-done-with.
58. Clark, A. (2015). 16 facts that show how going vegan helps stop climate change *PETA UK.* https://www.peta.org.uk/blog/how-going-vegan-helps-stop-climate-change/.
59. Moncrief, D. (2012). *A Well Fed World.* https://responsibleeatingandliving.com/favorites/dawn-moncrieffe-212012-interview/. Cited 20/10/2019
60. Donnelly, J. (2017). *BBC British History in Depth: The Irish Famine.* Bbc.Co.Uk. https://www.bbc.co.uk/history/british/victorians/famine_01.shtml.
61. Triodos Bank. (2019). *Conscious consumerism: What it means, why it's popular and how it's changing the world.* https://colour-of-money.co.uk/conscious-consumerism/.
62. Newkey-Burden, C. (2018). There's a Christmas crisis going on: No one wants to kill your dinner. *Guardian.* https://www.theguardian.com/commentisfree/2018/nov/19/christmas-crisis-kill-dinner-work-abattoir-industry-psychological-physical-damage.
63. Carroll, Lewis. (1865). *Alice In Wonderland.* New York, NY: Macmillan.
64. Orr, D. (2004). *Earth in mind: On education, environment, and the human prospect. 10th Anniversary Edition and Chapter 24.* Island Press.
65. Gould, S. (1991). *Enchanted evening.* Natural History (p. 14).
66. Wikipedia (2019). Jeffrey Dahmer. https://en.wikipedia.org/wiki/Jeffrey_Dahmer.
67. FXCM UK. (2019). *The History of Currency.* https://www.fxcm.com/uk/insights/the-history-of-currency/.
68. Fabulous Platform Shoes. (2019). *Shoe materials: What do all those symbols mean?* http://fabulousplatformshoes.com/shoe-materials-what-do-all-those-symbols-mean.
69. Volunteering Matters. (2016). *The true measure of any society can be found in how it treats its most vulnerable members.* https://volunteeringmatters.org.uk/true-measure-society-can-found-treats-vulnerable-members/.
70. GOV.UK. (2013). *Equality Act 2010: Guidance.* https://www.gov.uk/guidance/equality-act-2010-guidance.
71. GOV.UK. (2017). *Eligibility for the school milk subsidy scheme: Milk consumed from 1 August 2017.* https://www.gov.uk/guidance/eligibility-for-the-school-milk-subsidy-scheme-milk-consumed-from-1-august-2017.

72. Department of Health (2014). *Next steps for nursery milk government response.* https://assets.publishing.service.gov.uk/government/uploads/system/uploads/attachment_d.
73. Roth, R. (2009). *That's why we don't eat animals: A book about vegans, vegetarians, and all living things.* Berkeley, CA: North Atlantic Books.
74. Roth, R. (2012). *Vegan is Love.* Berkeley, CA: North Atlantic Books.
75. Tsabet, L. (2018). How many LGBT books do you have in your school library? *tes. com.* https://www.tes.com/news/how-many-lgbt-books-do-you-have-your-school-library.
76. Haupt, A. (2013). Michelle Obama speaks out against childhood obesity. *Health U.S. News.* https://health.usnews.com/health-news/health-wellness/articles/2013/03/11/michelle-obama-speaks-out-against-childhood-obesity.
77. Jamie's Food Revolution. (2018). Meals on Wheels gets a whole new meaning.../../../ Downloads/jamiesfoodrevolution.org. https://www.jamiesfoodrevolution.org/meals-on-wheels-gets-a-whole-new-meaning/.
78. Obama, M. (2018). *Becoming.* New York, NY: Crown Publishing Group.
79. Taft, C. (2017). *Millennial Vegan.* Danvers, MA: Vegan Publishers.
80. BBC. (2018). *"Killing Vegans" Response From Waitrose Magazine Editor.* https://www.bbc.co.uk/news/uk-politics-46024087.
81. Taft, C. (2016). *Why I'm a pro-intersectional animal advocate. Vegan Publishers.* https://veganpublishers.com/intersectional
82. Institute for Humane Education. (2016). *The world becomes what we teach.* https://humaneeducation.org/resources/2016/the-world-becomes-what-we-teach-book/.
83. Finnish National Agency for Education. (2019). *Finnish education system.* https://www.oph.fi/en/education-system.
84. Unti, B., & DeRosa, B. (2003). Humane education: Past, present, and future. In D.J. Salem & A.N. Rowan (Eds.), *The state of the animals II: 2003* (pp. 27-50). Washington, DC: Humane Society Press.